A WORLDLY SPIRITUALITY

A WORLDLY SPIRITUALITY

The Call to Redeem Life on Earth

Wesley Granberg-Michaelson

Harper & Row, Publishers, San Francisco
Cambridge, Hagerstown, New York, Philadelphia
London, Mexico City, São Paulo, Singapore, Sydney

For Karin, Jon Krister, and Karis Rose

FIRST EDITION

Library of Congress Cataloging in Publication Data

Granberg-Michaelson, Wesley.
    A WORLDLY SPIRITUALITY.

    Bibliography: p.
    Includes index.
    1. Church and the world. 2. Human ecology—Religious aspects—Christianity. 3. Church and social problems.
    I. Title.
BR115.W6G69   1984   261.8'362   83-48997
ISBN 0-06-063380-8

84 85 86 87 88 10 9 8 7 6 5 4 3 2 1

Contents

Introductory Note

SENATOR MARK HATFIELD

Seldom in my reading of Christian literature have I encountered such thought-provoking questions as I did in *A Worldly Spirituality*. Treading on virgin soil, Wesley Granberg-Michaelson focuses on crucial, yet long-ignored, aspects of Christian stewardship that must be addressed as we hope for a livable future.

Granberg-Michaelson examines the Creation and the Fall in an effort to find our proper, responsible role in God's creation. He thoroughly analyzes the condition of the world and suggests frightening projections of what troubles we will encounter if we pursue our current, rapidly abusing pace.

Standard Christian dogma is examined and often questioned in this book. Why do Christians who respond to God's call to "have dominion over" and "subdue the earth" neglect and misuse the world, rather than have a sincere concern for its future? Is a commonly held theological belief that "the second coming of Christ negates any reason to improve or even preserve the existing world" sound? Or are there alternative ways to view Christian stewardship? *A Worldly Spirituality* challenges us with the view that we are all (animals, land, water, as well as humans) a part of the entire creation and that we exist for His pleasure. Our responsibilities as Christians are certainly not limited to servanthood among humanity—rather, the task is magnified to stewardship of the whole universe.

As I studied the pages of this book, I frequently paused in my reading to grapple with the thought-provoking insights found in Granberg-Michaelson's writing. Scriptures that before had limited application for me suddenly sprang forth with more freshness and meaning. My understanding of stewardship grew from the insightful chapters of this book.

Granberg-Michaelson exposes us to questions that many of us will address for the first time. I continue to be grateful for Wes's contribution to my thinking and his challenge to integrate what I believe with difficult policy choices on military and resource issues. My prayer is that this book will undermine the misguided notion that the world's resources are infinite and that they are merely toys to abuse or neglect as we see fit. We are encouraged by *A Worldly Spirituality* to become Christian stewards who wisely view the world as God's beautiful but limited creation.

Foreword

JEREMY RIFKIN

We live in a time punctuated by a shared sense of endings. If there is a common theme to the current era, it would have to be the dominating presence of the word *survival*. Our personal lives, the life of our society, our civilization, and our species, lie precariously near the edge of history. We live in the shadow of the bomb and under the darker shadow of our own failed attempts as a social animal. We sense that we are edging closer to a tragic loss of unimaginable dimensions; yet we feel helplessly unable to stir the consciousness of the race away from the vision of a great planetary firestorm—a vision that has beckoned us since the first cloud of dust swooped skyward from the ashen debris of the ancient Japanese countryside.

The bomb serves as the ultimate expression of our unsociability. It is a dramatic testimonial to our increasing inability to relate to one another. We have become awkward with ourselves and uncomfortable with the world we have created. Where once we strutted across entire continents assured of our right to tame the earth to our own liking, now we hesitate, even founder. Where once we gloried in each new technological triumph, convinced that every increment would bring us closer to the completion of our own earthly Eden, now we shudder at the mere thought of our technological prowess. Still we, the children of Adam and Eve, continue to borrow from the tree of knowledge, dishing up an ever richer diet of technological fruits, each more powerful and expropriating, each less respectful of the creation from which they were fashioned and to which they are beholden. And with each passing day we become more proficient and less sociable, more accomplished with our tools and less sure of our goals, more skilled at manipulating our environment and less at ease with our surroundings.

The source of our discomfort lies deeply buried in the psyche of the race. If the products of our own handiwork appear to be more and more menacing to the pulsebeat of life, it is because the thinking that went into them has been jaded and warped by a false sense of our role in the great scheme of things. We experience a world divided and shattered. Life against life, community against community. We have spent the millennia of our existence in frenzied pursuit of control over all things, including each other. We have sought the knowledge of expropriation and lusted for power over the tiniest details and largest outlines of our environment.

From the very first day of our expatriation from the Garden of Paradise, we have lived by a creed that is at odds with God's mandate for his children. For as long as anyone cares to remember, we have used our great gift, the human mind, to pursue a very circumscribed existence. If there has been a watchword guiding the affairs of the race, it would be the belief that knowledge is power, power is control, and control is security. Our species has dedicated itself to a singular mission: to become the master over all things. In fact, we have for so long been preoccupied with the drive for power that we are barely able to imagine any other way to exercise the consciousness of the race. That is why we find it so terribly difficult to extricate ourselves from the death march we are presently on. The path that leads to the apocalypse is the path of power, a course that we have chosen for ourselves since the beginning of our history.

It is power that separates. It is power that severs relationships. If the world is hopelessly divided against itself it is because we have sliced and cut our way through the latticework of life, leaving in shambles what was once an indivisible whole. We now find ourselves the sovereign rulers over a scarred and ravaged sphere. The anatomy of the planet weakens daily. It groans under the travail that we have subjected it to. Our victory over the forces of nature has proven to be rather hollow. What, indeed, have we gained in the long march to power? Certainly not the security we have long sought after. Each day we find new, more ingenious ways to greater power, and each day we feel more insecure and helpless in the face of the social and technological forces we have unleashed.

If there was ever a time to reask the primordial question, Why human existence? surely that time must be now. If we are to avoid the final, deadly outcome of our own Promethian hubris, we must be prepared to reopen an examination of first causes. If we have strayed, we must investigate the time, place, and circumstances of our journey into darkness. If we are to find our way back to the Garden, we need to know how to rechart our course.

Wesley Granberg-Michaelson brings us back to the beginning of our story: to Genesis, and to God's first instructions to our kind. It is here that we must look, according to the author, if we are to find the answers we so desperately need to recast the fortunes of the race and the planet we're housed on.

Granberg-Michaelson's treatise is as much an exercise in language as it is a source of theological inspiration. The author asks us to reconsider definitions and interpretations. Nothing could be more important. As we know, first there was the word. We live by words. They define our existence. Each word is a contract. It binds together every individual into an insoluble community. Every time a word is uttered and accepted by another, a mutual partnership is formed. By sharing words we share experiences. We forge common bonds. Granberg-Michaelson asks us to look with fresh eyes at the first words uttered by the great Jehovah. God said to Adam and Eve, "You shall have dominion over the fish of the sea, the fowl of the air, and over every living thing that crawls upon the earth." Is it possible that we have somehow misread those words? Have we, in fact, misinterpreted the very first message ever conveyed? *A Worldly Spirituality* is about redefining our terms and finding our way back to the covenant God made with the first of our kind. The author provides humanity with a new way to listen to that timeless voice that pervades the universe. What we begin to hear is old words with new meanings. Words that excite our imagination. Words that encourage and heal. Words that reunite long-severed connections. Words that inspire a new vision and sense of purpose.

The message of this book is uncomplicated, yet earthshaking in its implications. Granberg-Michaelson serves us all as teacher and prophet, scribe and activist. If his fundamental reinterpretation of

biblical doctrine takes hold in the body of the church, it is possible
to conceive of a great spiritual metamorphosis within the Judeo-
Christian world: a transformation that can begin to heal the gaping
wounds we have inflicted on the whole of creation. The first step
toward liberation from our own self-imposed bondage is to care
enough to listen with new ears to the ancient biblical teachings.
Granberg-Michaelson's work provides a beginning for a new beginning.

Preface

It is common for authors to acknowledge their gratitude to various people and institutions that have made possible the writing of a book. For my part, this book represents the completion of thoughts and stirrings which began several years ago. Along the way in my Christian pilgrimage I have found the support of Christian community to be indispensable in both exploring and trying to live out my understanding of biblical faith. My experience in Christian community began with the Church of the Saviour and was furthered by my participation in the Sojourners Fellowship, both of which are in Washington, D.C. Since 1980 I have been part of the Community Covenant Church in Missoula, Montana. My deepest gratitude goes towards all the members of these communities with whom I have shared thought and life. What I have expressed on these pages would have been impossible without the nurture and corporate reflection of these faith communities.

Ideas are rarely either original or individual. Rather, they emerge out of the fabric of life and relationships. Thus the thoughts in this book merely reflect a rich tapestry of insight from many other authors and friends. I have tried to acknowledge these wherever possible.

I am grateful in particular to Western Theological Seminary in Holland, Michigan, where I served as scholar-in-residence for six months while doing much of the work on this manuscript. Its faculty, staff, and students provided an atmosphere of warm hospitality and offered opportunities for reflection on many of the ideas in the manuscript. In particular, Lester Kuyper, Chris Kaiser, and Bill Scudder spent many hours with me in fruitful conversation.

The AuSable Trails Institute of Environmental Studies in Mancelona, Michigan, provided several opportunities for very useful reflection on the subject of this book during conferences held there over the past three years.

Sharon Murfin not only typed the manuscript but has been a source of deep encouragement to me in her faithful service and friendship.

Finally, while writing this book I have tried to be a very involved father to our young son, Jon Krister. In this process my wife, Karin, and I have worked hard to balance the joys of parenting with the time necessary for vocation. I thank her, not only for her constant support, but for the style of life we have tried to develop to ensure that getting ideas in print need not diminish the nurturing love within a family.

I. THE PERIL: CREATION DESTROYED

1. The Plight of the Earth

Civilization imperils the creation. Humanity is arrogantly seizing the prerogatives of the creator. The desire to be like God, while present since the fall, is becoming a technological possibility. Never have the consequences of humanity's growing domination over nature been so alarming, and so potentially devastating.

Humanity now possesses the power actually to destroy the created world. For thousands of years of human history, people were beset by the fear that the gods might destroy the world. But what the gods have spared, humanity itself can now obliterate. We now stand in fear of human rather than divine power.

Humanity's arsenals of nuclear destruction lie at the heart of creation's ecological crisis. The common tendency to treat the nuclear threat and environmental concerns as separate issues is seriously mistaken, and promotes a narrow-mindedness toward both matters. Unlike past technologies of war, aimed at destroying opposing armies, industrial capacities, or populations, nuclear war unleashes its power against the very life of creation. And the ability to end that life is now within humanity's grasp.

Technology is also enabling humanity to create life. An unprecedented ability to manufacture new forms of life has emerged in scientific laboratories. In 1980, the U.S. Supreme Court ruled that new forms of genetically engineered life could be granted patents. Within two years, over one hundred and fifty genetic engineering firms were established, many with the enthusiastic backing and capital of Wall Street.

The inexorable evolution of genetic engineering is moving from the creation of micro-organisms with industrial uses toward the potential of genetically engineering a human being to desired specifications. New life forms are being introduced into the environment, and species lines are suddenly being blurred. Noah cared for the species two by two, to ensure life's continuity. Today humanity can nearly create new species to satisfy its whims or to generate a return on an investment.

Biotechnology's stock has risen because of its promises to produce hormones, enzymes, and drugs, to create organisms that will gobble up oil spills, to enable plants to take their nitrogen from the atmosphere, to cure genetic defects in humans, and other much heralded pledges. But in the process, life itself is being redefined to suit humanity's new mastery over the creation. Jeremy Rifkin describes in his book *Algeny* how separate species with separate names are gradually being seen as systems of information that can be reprogrammed into an endless number of biological combinations. "Life as information flow represents the final desacralization of nature,"[1] he notes.

When the federal courts were considering whether the new forms of life "owned" by Upjohn and General Electric could be patented, those supporting the patents argued that the "life" of these micro-organisms was negligible; no more than physical and chemical elements were involved, which were just as patentable as a ball bearing. Genentech, a trail-blazing genetic engineering firm, filed an *amicus* brief with the courts that quoted Claude Bernard a century ago; he distinguished three kinds of properties exhibited by living beings: physical properties, chemical properties, and vital properties. Properties that have not been reduced to physio-chemical terms are those referred to as "vital." But this was only provisional, according to Bernard, until such time as scientists succeed in unlocking the secret of these properties.[2]

Something startling is happening here. As life itself is commercialized, it is defined only according to its material characteristics. The vital, sacred, and reverential qualities of life evaporate. We are left simply with a vast new pool of "material" to be technologically manipulated into forms of economic utility.

Dr. Leon Kass, a molecular biologist and author, believes we have paid a high price for the technological conquest of nature; he cites the intellectual and spiritual costs of our coming to see nature as merely something to manipulate. Kass remarks that "with the powers for biological engineering now gathering, there will be splendid new opportunities for a similar degradation of our view of man."[3]

The future possibilities of the bioengineering of life are being set not by moral or theological judgments, nor by governmental guidelines, but simply by economic feasibilities. The biochip seems destined to replace the microchip as the technological icon of a new age. Humanity now has the power to re-create the fabric of life, including the life of the human species. As with nuclear power, the consequences of this capacity are awesome, and without precedent in human history.

Liebe F. Cavalieri, professor of biochemistry at Cornell Medical College, has sensed this parallel between nuclear science and genetic engineering and voices his concern that while molecular biologists, like nuclear physicists before them, are pleased to have revealed another of nature's secrets, genetic engineering is not just another scientific advance. "Like nuclear physics," he states, "it confers on human beings a power for which they are psychologically and morally unprepared. The physicists have already learned this, to their dismay; the biologists, not yet."[4]

With its contemporary technological ability to destroy and create life, humanity is striving to replace God as the ruler over creation.

Humanity's mastery over nature has already resulted in a persistent deterioration in the earth's ecosphere, threatening its life-supporting capacity. Some cultures have conceived of all things as being comprised of four elements—earth, water, air, and fire (energy). Analyzing the contemporary condition of each one of these four elements reveals the precarious condition with regard to creation's ability to support life.

EARTH

Luxury homes and condominiums have erased half a million of Michigan's cherry trees in the past six years. The Old Mission Peninsula overlooking Grand Traverse Bay possesses a climate and soil perfectly suited for producing nearly three-quarters of the nation's tart cherries. But in recent years mortgage payments from new housing developments have been the fastest growing harvest from those slopes.

In Flemington, New Jersey, eighty-year-old John Case, who has raised chickens on his 270 acres since 1930, hears complaints from new suburban neighbors that his farm is spreading flies. Despite passing inspections from county and state health department officials, Case's farm is threatened by the growth of suburbia. In 1950, 13 million chickens populated New Jersey. Two decades later, there were fewer than 2 million.

Even in the U.S. West, where land seems to extend as far as the sky, farming is steadily giving ground to subdivisions, strip-mining, highways, energy development, and urban sprawl. Near my home in Montana's Missoula County, over four hundred residents listed agriculture as their chief source of income in 1970. Today, fewer than a hundred do.

If Montana's rate of agricultural land loss from 1967 to 1977 continues to the end of the century, almost one quarter of all its prime farmland will be gone. Half of Massachusetts' prime land will be lost. And nearly all of Florida's prime farmland, which produces half of the world's grapefruits and one quarter of its oranges, will disappear if that state's present trends continue.

Agricultural land in the United States is being lost at the rate of 3 million acres per year, according to the federal government's National Agricultural Lands Study completed in early 1981.[5] Often this includes prime agricultural land, which is converted into housing developments, industrial uses, energy mining and production, and other nonagricultural purposes.

At the same time, the demand for production from agricultural land is increasing. Estimates suggest that to meet domestic as well as international food needs, an additional 85 to 140 million acres of land need to be cultivated in the United States before the end of the century.

Many experts predict that in the next decades, the shortage of farmland will pose as serious a concern to North Americans as the shortage of gas and oil in the 1970s. Food and farmland could well become the central natural resource question of the next decade.

As farmland in the United States decreases, our food needs will increasingly be met by cash crops raised in Third World countries for export to affluent countries. This will result in less land for food to meet the needs of the hungry within their own borders.

Compounding the problem of land loss in the United States is the changing structure of agriculture and shifting patterns of ownership of agricultural lands. Over two-thirds of all farms in the United States have disappeared since 1920.[6] A U.S. Senate committee found that today, half of all America's farmland is actually farmed by nonowners. The U.S. Department of Agriculture projects that while the overall number of farms will decrease by 35 percent in the next two decades, the number of large farms will quadruple. Because of such trends, by the end of the century half of all the farmland in the United States will be owned by only 3 percent of America's farmers.

The rising cost of farmland is the central factor in this changing pattern of ownership. In 1970, the average value of a farmland acre was $196. In early 1980, it was $641, with continuing increases since then. Added to this are enormous capital costs for machinery, fuel, fertilizers, and commonly used pesticides. As a result, prospective new farmers find it difficult, if not impossible, to afford farming, and today's farmers are driven deeper into debt—a debt that averages $68,000 today per farmer. Wealthy farmers as well as investors, banks, and insurance companies are purchasing most farmland sold today.

The Prudential Insurance Company of America owned 100,000 acres of farmland two years ago. Today it owns almost 600,000 acres. Over half of U.S. farmland has changed ownership in the past two decades. The consolidation of land ownership into fewer, richer hands is a worrisome and threatening trend. The care of the earth as a resource given by God is far better entrusted to those who live close to the land and depend on it, rather than upon impersonal economic forces that deal with land simply as a financial investment.

Land is also being lost at accelerating rates to erosion from wind and water, posing a major threat to both the quality and quantity of agricultural soil. Since tillage agriculture began in North America with white settlers, one-third of our topsoil has been permanently lost. Presently, 100 million acres of farmland in the United States are being eroded at the rate of eight tons per year, far more acreage than can be renewed by nature. And much of this is within the Corn Belt, which holds some of the nation's most productive soil.

The Empty Breadbasket? an intensive study of the U.S. food system produced by the Cornucopia Project of Rodale Press, reported that the annual loss of topsoil by erosion is 6.4 billion tons, "more than enough to cover all the cropland in the New England states of Maine, New Hampshire, Vermont, Massachusetts, Connecticut, and Rhode Island, plus New York, New Jersey, Pennsylvania, Delaware, Maryland, Alabama, Arizona, California, and Florida with over one inch of dirt."[7] According to the report, the United States is losing 25 percent more soil today than it lost during the dust bowl times in the 1930s.[8]

Erosion and development remove thirty-four square miles of agriculturally productive soil from the United States every day— an amount of soil that could provide a yearly minimum diet for 260,000 people.[9]

The decline of organic material in soil, caused by the massive use of synthetic fertilizers, is also increasing the rate of soil deterioration and erosion. And reduced organic material, or humus, in the soil increases the release of carbon dioxide into the atmosphere, contributing to a potentially disastrous temperature rise in the earth's atmostphere.

Finally, the nation's demand for new energy sources poses major threats to agriculture. Some of the land that formerly produced food for our stomachs now produces fuel for our cars. And, although the use of agricultural wastes for making alcohol fuels can be wise and energy efficient, converting vast acres into fuel-producing rather than food-producing cropland means the mobility of the rich may in the long run contribute to the hunger of the poor.

In the resource-rich West, energy development conflicts sharply with agriculture. A stable and productive rural culture is being threatened by the new Western coal rush. One Montana rancher asks, "How do I pass a strip mine on to my kids?" Water, the lifeline of Western agriculture, is in short supply; it is also coveted by those planning oil shale development, coal slurry pipelines, and other energy development techniques.

Beneath all these alarming trends is the erosion of a land ethic. We are losing not merely land as a resource for food; we are losing our relationship to the land as its caretakers and servants. The traditions of rural life, along with the sense of stewardship of the earth, are being eroded. Increasingly, land is becoming a mere commodity to be bought and sold, rather than a treasure to be nurtured, cared for, and utilized in the service of meeting the needs of all people.

R. Neil Sampson, Executive Vice-President of the National Association of Conservation Districts, has stated that we are in need of a new land ethic, a change in our thinking about the care and use of this vital resource, and that this can be accomplished only through education and social evolution.[10]

The threats to the land base of the earth are evident not merely in the United States, but throughout the globe. In the world's poorer countries, deforestation and desertification—the evolving of once fertile land areas into desert regions—is destroying the productive capacity and genetic resources of vast areas of the earth.

In portions of East Africa, for instance, the search for firewood, the chief energy source for millions of people, combined with the overgrazing of marginal lands, is causing the desert to expand and the soil to deteriorate in ways that may be irreversible. The World Bank has actually projected a continuing decline in per capita income for the impoverished residents in much of sub–Saharan Africa. A deteriorating environment, in such a case, leads quickly and directly to eroding the very meager livelihood of millions of the world's poor.

The Global 2000 Report to the President, originated by the Carter

Administration in 1977 and completed in 1980, reported that forests and commercial wood in less-developed countries would be depleted by 40 percent by the year 2000.[12] Ninety percent of such wood is used for heating and cooking. By 2020, or less than two generations from now, nearly all the accessible forests in those parts of the world will have been cut.[13]

Not only will this deprive the world's poor of their basic energy source: as anyone who has looked at a clear-cut hillside knows, trees soak up moisture, helping to regulate the flow of water across the land, and deter the erosion of soil. The widespread elimination of forests leads to the loss of soil.

In tropical regions, lush rainforests are being cut and burned away at such a rapid rate that cries of alarm have been heard from scientists and research groups around the world. The Amazon region is experiencing the most devastating levels of tropical deforestation. Warnings have been sounded concerning the potential increase of carbon dioxide in the earth's atmosphere from the elimination of such vast quantities of plant life, in addition to the loss of soil productivity.

More seriously, such deforestation results in the dramatic extinction of plant and insect species. The United Nations has reported that 10 percent of all flowering plants are now "dangerously rare,"[14] due in large part to the 11 million hectares of tropical forests that are destroyed each year. Some scientists estimate that another species of plant or animal life becomes extinct from the earth every hour. All this depletes the genetic resources and biological diversity that are fundamental to nurturing the process of life.

Ghillean Prance, Vice-President of the New York Botanical Gardens and a leading expert on tropical rainforests, told a congressional committee that despite all the reports of these severe dangers posed by tropical deforestation, "the destruction has continued unabated. It has not eased off at all."[15]

In 1955, the so-called less-developed countries possessed a little under half a hectare of arable land for each person. By the year

2000, those nations will have only one-fifth of a hectare of productive land for each of their inhabitants.[16]

Both the quality and quantity of land from the good earth, which sustains not only humanity but also the globe's ecosphere, are diminishing more rapidly than at any previous time since humanity began tilling the soil. Keeping the earth—preserving that thin membrane of soil so crucial to the life of the planet—has never been so urgent a calling.

WATER

Water has been thought to be abundant and free. While limitations in other world resources have been accepted, few believe that water could ever be a scarce global commodity. Yet, it is becoming so.

The area around Pecos, Texas, flourished ten years ago, with a thousand farmers growing cotton on irrigated land. But because the water table fell and energy prices for pumping up the water increased, most of those farms today are desolate. The Ogallala aquifer (a natural underground reservoir) stretches from the Texas Panhandle to South Dakota. In some areas, water used primarily for irrigation is being drained off the aquifer at fifteen to eighteen times the rate that nature replenishes it.[17]

Just like oil or copper, water is being mined, and its supply is finite. The Ogallala aquifer has no more than forty years of life left; yet the farming economies of western Kansas, Nebraska, and the Texas Panhandle are founded on the assumption that there is abundant water for irrigation. The economic effects of a dropping water table are already rippling through the Great Plains.

Eighty-one percent of the water consumed in the United States is used for irrigation, mostly in the West.[18] Since the 1930s, much water used for irrigation has been pumped out of the ground from aquifers. Many of those areas relying on groundwater irrigation are facing the prospect of water shortages.

Even surface water flowing through rivers and streams and used for irrigation and other purposes is in short supply. With the ground water supply to cities like Tuscon and Phoenix facing depletion, the Central Arizona Project will divert Arizona's allotted share of water from the Colorado River to those areas, at a cost of $1.7 billion. California, which presently uses Colorado River water to irrigate 3 million acres of the Imperial Valley, is advancing billion dollar projects to pump water down from its own northern counties or elsewhere.[19] The 1963 Supreme Court ruling that divided up water from the Colorado to various states actually allocated more water than flows in the Colorado River—a reality that will probably become evident by 1985.[20]

Further, the pressures for massive energy development throughout the West put additional demands on already scarce water. Agriculture and energy development are becoming rivals in many western states as each compete for the limited water of the region.

Development that eliminates wetlands also dimishes water supply. For instance, few wetlands remain in Dade and Broward counties in South Florida, and development has spread through the East Everglades. One function of wetlands is to provide for a filtered resupply of water to aquifers. Development in south Florida and the water usages of the Miami area are causing the Biscayne aquifer to drop rapidly and sea water to seep in.[21]

While water for irrigation is becoming scarce in parts of the United States, water for drinking is becoming contaminated. According to the Environmental Protection Agency, the U.S. now generates 77 billion pounds of hazardous chemical wastes each year. Only an estimated 10 percent is disposed of in a thoroughly safe manner.[22]

Most water treatment facilities concentrate on eliminating bacteria, parasites, and viruses from the water. The effects of an estimated seven hundred organic chemicals in our drinking water are only beginning to be understood, and these are generally not controlled. Regulatory efforts have focused on trying to prevent disasters like the Love Canal, controlling the pollution of surface water from specific points, such as an industrial plant. But an estimated half of all pollutants come from other, more diffuse sources.

Determined efforts could remedy the pollution of surface waters. The most serious threat to safe drinking water comes from the chemical wastes improperly dumped or buried that seep into the ground and contaminate groundwater, which supplies half of U.S. drinking water. Once groundwater is polluted, little can be done but to close up wells. The Cornucopia Project reported that a spot check by EPA of over eight thousand hazardous waste disposal sites revealed that almost three-fourths were nothing more than a hole in the ground, and seven hundred of these were within a mile of wells used for drinking water.[23]

Neither the quantity nor the quality of water in the United States can be taken for granted any longer, and globally the picture presents further reasons for alarm.

Nearly half the countries in the world will experience a doubling in their demand for water by the year 2000 from population growth alone. Several of these are poor countries where the per capita use of water is already low, and where improvement in living conditions would require water use to increase by several times. Thus, many nations most in need of more water will be least able to get it. The *Global 2000 Report* lists a number of countries whose per capita water availability will be "very low" by the year 2000, including South Korea, Syria, countries on the Arabian Peninsula, Pakistan, Bangladesh, Tunisia, Algeria, Morocco, Egypt, West Sahara, Rwanda, Burundi, Malawi, Jamaica, and Haiti.[24]

The largest worldwide use of water is for irrigation. But while making land fertile to grow food, irrigation also causes negative side effects now being experienced globally. Salt, found in all water, condenses as irrigated water evaporates. It then either collects in the soil or washes into surface or groundwater. Although this is a normal porcess in nature, irrigation can vastly accelerate it, increasing the salinity of the water and the land, and reducing crop yields by up to 50 percent or more.

In Pakistan, almost three-quarters of its irrigated land suffers from salinity and other irrigation-related problems. Five million acres along the Indus River have nearly been ruined. A total of about half of all the world's irrigated land has been damaged by salinization, as well as waterlogging and alkalinization.[25]

The quality of water for drinking has also become a global problem. The United Nations Environment Programme's report, "The State of the World Environment, 1972–1982," observed that "the absolute numbers of people without access to safe drinking water increased"[26] over that decade. And a World Health Organization survey of drinking water supplies and hygenic waste disposal, covering people in eighty-eight developing countries, found that 77 percent of the people were not being adequately served.[27]

The *Global 2000 Report* summarized the future of the world water supply in this manner:

Any significant increase in the rate of water withdrawal, even a doubling by the year 2000, is virtually certain to cause major water supply problems. . . . Water shortages will become more frequent, and their effects will be more widespread and severe. . . . The notion of water as a free good available in essentially limitless quantities will have disappeared throughout much of the world.[28]

AIR

Air that is clean, breathable, and capable of regenerating the creation could be in short supply in the years ahead. In North America, acid rain respects no borders; it has poisoned thousands of lakes in eastern Canada and the United States. Plans in the United States to increase the burning of coal in order to generate electricity threaten to intensify the levels of acid rain.

North American air in many regions holds high levels of pollutants called fine particles, which present special hazards because they can be drawn deeply into the lungs. Our air also contains scores of toxic chemical pollutants. Many scientists agree that various of these toxic chemicals are responsible for causing cancer; controlling them is an essential step in the fight to prevent cancer.

Yet by 1982, the Environmental Protection Agency had set controls on only four toxic chemicals. Thirty-seven other toxic chemicals suspected of causing cancer or other diseases had been studied, but no action had been taken. Only aggressive steps by the Congress in rewriting the Clean Air Act and resistance to Reagan Administration efforts to weaken the law prevented a further deterioration in the quality of our air.

That act, first passed in 1970, demonstrated that some environmental threats can be solved by well-directed governmental actions. In the decade that followed, carbon monoxide levels declined by 35 percent because of controls set by that law on auto emissions. Between 1964 and 1977, sulfur dioxide levels in the U.S. atmosphere decreased by 65 percent. Many cities actually showed an improvement in air quality.

Yet there is no room for breathing easy. Acid rain and toxic pollutants still poison our lungs, lakes, and lands. Diesel cars, trucks, and buses are flooding the highways, with engines that emit thirty to seventy times more particulate matter (pollution) than gas engines. Additional controls on cars, to be in effect by 1985, would still result in diesel engines that spew out fifteen times more pollutants than their gasoline counterparts.[29] And plans for vastly increasing the burning of coal threatens the air with increased pollutants as well as a potentially catastrophic increase in the earth's temperature.

A 1982 Harris poll showed that an overwhelming 84 percent of Americans favored retaining or strengthening the Clean Air Act. Such strong public opinion only narrowly prevented the Reagan Administration and industrial interests from severely weakening and dismantling the Clean Air Act in 1982. Those protecting clean air had to battle on the defensive, while threats to air quality from politicians and pollutants continued to grow.

Since the United Nations Environment Conference in Stockholm in 1982, scientific concern over three threats to the earth's atmosphere has increased: the rising level of carbon dioxide, the depletion of the ozone layer in the upper atmosphere, and the increase of acid rain throughout the globe.

The level of carbon dioxide in the earth's atmosphere has increased by fifteen percent in the last century. By the year 2000, there may be a third more CO_2 in the earth's air than in pre-industrial time, and according to the projected increase of fossil fuel burning, carbon dioxide in the atmosphere will double by the middle of the next century.[30] That doubling will actually occur sooner in all likelihood, due to the rapid devastation of tropical forests mentioned earlier.

What will result? Doubling the level of CO_2 will increase the atmosphere's temperature by two to three degrees centigrade in the middle latitudes of the earth. The effects on climate, precipitation, and agriculture would be enormous. Such a warming trend would exceed any temperature change that has taken place naturally on the earth in the last ten thousand years.[31]

The temperature rise would be three to four times greater at the poles of the earth than toward the equator. A rise of only five to ten degrees centigrade in those areas would eventually melt the Antarctic and Greenland icecaps. The gradual rise in sea level would engulf many coastal cities throughout the globe.[32]

The added dimension to this as well as other threats to the earth's atmosphere is that humanity cannot simply wait to see the effects before changing its actions. By then it will be too late. We will have no thermostat to turn down.

The depletion of the ozone layer presents a similar problem. Ozone in the upper atmosphere protects the earth from the damaging effects of ultraviolet light on plants, animals, ecosystems, and humans, in whom it may cause skin cancer. Chlorofluorocarbons released by aerosol spray cans and refrigeration equipment, as well as nitrous oxide emissions from the use of nitrogen fertilizers, deplete the ozone layer. Estimates and calculations are understandably imprecise.

Dr. Michael Oppenheimer, Senior Scientist for the Environmental Defense Fund, told Congress that if current depletion rates continue, 5 percent to 9 percent of the ozone layer would be lost by the end of the century.[33] The United Nations Environmental Programme predicted a 10 percent depletion of ozone by 2050.[34] And although aerosol cans in the United States have decreased in use, those improvements have been offset by an increase in the other known causes of ozone depletion.

Changing the basic character of the earth's atmosphere even slightly presents great and largely unknown risks to the ecosphere. Removing ozone from the upper atmosphere is an irreversible process that could substantially cripple the earth's delicately balanced life-supporting functions.

Acid rain devastates not only North America, but much of the globe. Fifteen hundred lakes in southern Norway are now acidified, and 70 percent no longer support fish. Growing acid levels in many Norwegian rivers have eliminated the salmon and trout.[35] While the effects of acid rain on water have been most studied, it also damages soils, crops, and forests. Apart from North America and Scandinavia, acid rain is also projected to increase over many areas of Germany, Eastern Europe, and the Soviet Union, due primarily to fossil fuel combustion, as well as the smelting of certain sulfur-bearing ores.

As in other areas of air quality, the problem is not primarily technological, but political. Technological solutions to significantly reduce sulfur emissions and curtail acid rain are resisted because of their cost, and the failure of politicians to override narrow interests.

The earth's atmosphere is being steadily subjected to attacks that seriously jeopardize its basic, life-giving character. The chief offenders are the most industrialized countries, with the United States leading the way as the "largest single producer of these atmospheric perturbations."[36] What is required, in Dr. Oppenheimer's words, is "an international effort to manage our atmospheric resource, treating clean air as a scarce commodity."[37]

ENERGY (FIRE)

By discovering and harnessing fire, humanity learned how to use energy stored in materials on and under the earth for keeping warm, cooking food, and eventually for transportation and the building of an industrialized society. While pre-industrial society used wood as its basic commodity not only for heating but also for its tools, ships, wagons, carts, and such technological inventions as looms and oil presses, industrialized society is built on fossil fuels.

The extent of modern society's dependence on petroleum and its by-products is staggering. We heat, eat, and travel largely by oil and coal; most of our clothes are synthetic fabrics dependent on petroleum, as are the plastics and related products that fill our homes and stores. The heat to smelt, fabricate, and produce the materials with which we construct our society, and the electricity to run and light it, depend heavily on fossil fuels. That is why a shortage in this source of stored energy has potentially devastating effects on modern industrialized life.

The popular picture of the energy crisis shows us using the last barrel of available oil, and assurances by oil industry officials and some politicians that much more oil remains to be discovered have largely quieted public fears of any imminent energy catastrophe. Shortages, however, begin to be noticed not when the commodity has run out, but when demand for it becomes greater than the available supply. Several studies predict that such a crunch in the oil supply will occur before the year 2000, and perhaps before the end of the 1980s.[38] A situation in which the demand for oil begins to markedly exceed supply, with continuing sharp rises in oil prices, could be hastened by several factors, including a decision by OPEC countries to put a ceiling on their production in order to stretch out the life of their oil supply.

Global production of oil, which is the world's leading energy source in use, will reach its peak before the century's end, and then begin to decline. The continuing climb in oil prices will have crippling results on the industrialized, oil-dependent economies. Increasingly, the prosperous will outbid the less fortunate in claiming this source of energy; but money will not be able to solve the problem of a dwindling supply.

What this means is that the world's chief source of energy must be replaced. In the words of the *Global 2000 Report to the President,* "A world transition away from petroleum dependence must take place, but there is still much uncertainty as to how this transition will occur."[39]

Conventional wisdom assumes that the industrialized societies will continue their reliance on centralized energy systems, using large power plants to produce electricity. The shortage in petroleum may be made up by the increased use of coal, which has more plentiful reserves, and added nuclear energy. This has been called the "hard energy path," and it also envisions the rapid development of synthetic fuels through coal-gasification projects, and major development of oil shale and coal tar resources.

Studies by the U.S. Department of Energy predict that the world's energy demand will increase by 58 percent from 1975 to 1990. If we project that same rate of increase to the end of the century, and assume that the world follows the hard energy path, we discover the enormous social and environmental costs that would result. One hundred billion tons of coal would have to be mined, thousands of square miles of land would be strip-mined, and thousands of square miles of additional land would be affected by subsidence, or land sinking. About one thousand coal power plants would be built around the world, along with several hundred more nuclear power plants. Tens of thousands of square miles would be required just for the transmission lines carrying the electric power from these plants to various locations. About a billion tons of radioactive tailings from supplying uranium would be produced, along with 10 million cubic meters of low-level radioactive wastes. In addition there would be several hundred thousand tons of spent nuclear fuel.[40]

These staggering totals do not include the global impact on air and water resources from increased coal burning. Carbon dioxide in the air would double by 1990, and by century's end the increase in atmospheric temperature could begin to disrupt seriously the earth's climate. Increased sulfur dioxide in the atmosphere would threaten serious damage to crops, vegetation, fish, and other biological life. Further, chemically reducing these sulfur emissions produces another environmental hazard from the dangerous chemical-rich sludge that results, and increased oxides of nitrogen as well as particulate emissions would make breathing more difficult for millions of people.[41] Finally, much of the coal development is planned for areas of the western United States, where water is already scarce. Mining the coal can disrupt the aquifers, and coal-fired power plants as well as synfuels development such as coal gasification projects place intolerable demands on the region's sparse water.

The social and environmental costs of such energy development have usually been regarded as "side effects" that must be solved or eased. Increasingly, however, they are looming as the *main effects* of the hard energy path, and ones without satisfactory solution. The costs to society and the world's environment of the hard energy path cannot be avoided, and are so damaging that they cannot be afforded.

These realities have begun to focus attention on an alternative soft energy path for industrialized nations. This emphasizes energy conservation and renewable energy resources such as solar power that are decentralized and rely on relatively low technology. Several thorough studies have concluded that such a soft energy path can be taken by modern nations.

The recently conducted "Solar Sweden Study" examined whether that nation could rely entirely on various forms of solar energy in the future. Done by an agency of the Swedish government, the study concluded that "by 2015 Sweden could shift entirely to solar energy without prohibitive costs and without major changes in lifestyles."[42]

The U.S. Department of Energy funded a parallel study for the State of California. It reached similar conclusions, finding that by 2025 it would be largely possible to run the society using indigenous, sustainable energy resources.[43] And while the soft energy path also has environmental consequences, such studies indicate clearly that they are mild compared to the devastating impact of the hard energy path.

The study on California came to the important conclusion that "energy policy for the long term should be shaped by the awareness that social-environmental costs, not exhaustion of resources, will limit the amount of human well-being derivable from energy."[44] In other words, future energy choices must be made not on the basis of how much coal there is, but on the amount of environmental damage that would result from burning coal as opposed to using renewable energy resources.

The U.S. government's Council on Environmental Quality looked at forty studies on hard and soft energy paths for the United States, and concluded that the massive increases in energy called for by the hard path are not necessary to maintain a healthy economy.[45] In fact, reversing normal economic wisdom, the Council concluded that low growth in energy is not only compatible with continuing economic growth, but that the soft path leads to reduced unemployment and lower inflation.

Hard-headed analysis is demonstrating that the soft, solar, decentralized renewable energy strategy is an achievable option for industrialized society. But it requires a decisive change, beginning immediately, in energy policy. And no such change is being made.

Present policies in the industrialized world project a continued reliance on hard-energy technology. And those policies are on a collision course with the well-being of the globe's environment.

The debate over hard versus soft energy paths chiefly concerns the affluent. The world's poor majority has already been deprived of access to most sources of fossil fuel energy in their daily lives. And this second global energy system, functioning among the world's impoverished citizens, is facing its own crisis.

The poorer the region, the more wood is used as a chief fuel for family cooking and heating. With kerosene and electricity an unaffordable option for millions, the pressure for a larger supply of wood has grown. Shortages of wood in many local areas have resulted, along with the harmful increases in soil erosion on denuded land.

The U.N. Food and Agriculture Organization has predicted a serious shortage of fuel wood in poorer countries, totalling 650 million cubic meters, or nearly a fourth of overall need, by the year 1994. Thus, the shortage of fuel wood, already present in several locations, will present the poor with a tragic and debilitating energy crisis in the years ahead.

Without wood, the poor turn to burning animal dung or the remains of crops for their fuel, if these are options. But this only compounds the tragedy. Dung and crop residues are their only sources for fertilizing the land. The poor are those least able to afford chemical fertilizers, and now they are forced to burn their organic fertilizers, which amounts to burning potential food and destroying their soil.[46] For example, a ton of cow dung has enough nutrients to produce fifty kilograms of grain. This can provide the needed nutrition for one person for four months. In India, nearly 70 million tons of cow dung are burned as fuel.[47]

There are alternatives. Simple stoves can help burn wood far more efficiently. Small biogas plants, which take the energy out of manure and wastes in the form of methane to be burned as fuel but leave in the nutrients, are in widespread use in China. And using the sun and wind, through appropriate technologies, for cooking, irrigating, and other needs holds great promise. But these options require commitment and often cooperation and initial funding from outside sources.

The world's rich and poor live within two different energy economies, separated by a widening gulf. By the year 2000, per capital energy use in the United States is projected at the rate of 422 million BTU's (British thermal units) each year. The poorer nations will have only 14 million BTU's per person.

The shortage of oil in affluent countries is prompting vastly increased uses of coal and nuclear power, which will create intolerable threats and injuries to world's environment. And the shortage of wood in less-developed countries is creating a downward spiral that eats away the land and increases poverty and starvation. Learning to use renewable energy could unite the energy destiny of both rich and poor, and offer humanity the opportunity of utilizing the power of fire without destroying our earthly home.

POPULATION

The drain on the earth's resources and the threats to the globe's environment will be vastly increased by the coming growth in the world's population. Today, there are four times more people living on earth than at the beginning of this century. And the world's population now doubles every thirty-eight years.

The years between now and the end of this century will see nearly a 50 percent increase in the number of people living at one time on earth, from 4.4 billion to over 6 billion, and the overall rate of growth in the world's population is not expected to decrease very much at all during that time. Over the last ten years, that rate did decline somewhat in Europe, South Asia, and Latin America, but increased in Africa. The *Global 2000 Report* projects that population will continue to be growing at some level in nearly every region of the world when we reach the end of this century.

Further, the population of the poorer nations of the world will increase faster than the rich. By the year 2000, nearly eight out of ten people alive will be making their homes in less developed, poorer countries.[49] Moreover, the gap between the rich and poor will widen in the coming two decades. Present trends offer no hope that the poor as a whole will rise out of their poverty on the coattails of the affluent. In fact, for every dollar increase in the per capita Gross National Product of poorer, developing countries that is projected by the year 2000, the per capita GNP of the industrialized nations will increase by twenty dollars.[50]

Population growth in poorer countries is accompanied by an even more dramatic transformation: the growing urbanization of the world's poor. Halfway through the twentieth century, only one city in the less-developed countries had a population over 4 million—Buenos Aires. By 1960 there were eight, and by 1980 twenty-two cities in the poorer countries of the globe exceeded 4 million, compared to only sixteen such cities in the industrialized world.

Because of this rapid trend, the population living in cities will double by the century's end. By that time, sixty-one cities will have populations over 4 million in less-developed countries, compared to about twenty-five in richer countries. The U.N. estimates that as many as eighteen cities in poorer nations will have populations exceeding 10 million people, including Mexico City, Calcutta, Bombay, Cairo, Jakarta, Delhi, Karachi, and Tehran, among others. [51]

Urban growth among the poorer nations makes a variety of

problems worse. Squatter settlements multiply, lacking safe water and sanitation. The demand for basic human services for food, health, and well-being easily exceeds what can be given. Specific damages to the environment increase dramatically from such urban concentrations. Yet the growth of such cities is largely caused by the even harsher and more hopeless conditions of many rural areas.

The Global 2000 Report to the President includes this sobering conclusion in describing life on earth at the end of this century:

> The gap between the richest and the poorest will have increased. By every measure of material welfare the study provides—per capita GNP and consumption of food, energy, and minerals—the gap will widen.[52]

CONCLUSION

The picture of humanity's devastating impact on the creation of God is grim. And the forecast for the future is even worse. Following its present course, humanity seems certain to rupture the creation in a catastrophic way. The earth, air, water, and fire that sustain the life of humanity and all creation are all in serious jeopardy.

A disastrous outcome is not inevitable, however. Hope remains. But that hope rests not on the development of new technological advances to remove the problems magically. Rather, that hope rests on dramatically transforming humanity's relationship to the creation. New values, understandings, and attitudes, which in turn will make possible fresh political and social changes at local, national, and international levels, can spring forth only from a fundamentally new relationship between humanity and creation. Nothing less will suffice.

Humanity, then, must discover its intended relationship to the earth and its resources. And that is a religious search. Its answers are rooted in an encounter with the Creator.

NOTES

1. Jeremy Rifkin, *Algeny* (New York: Viking Press, 1983), p. 229.
2. Quoted in amicus brief on behalf of the People's Business Commission, *Amicus Curiae,* titled "The Case Against Patenting Life," Mo. 79–136, pp. 28–29.
3. Leon Kass, "Making Babies—The New Biology and the 'Old' Morality," *The Public Interest,* Winter 1972, quoted ibid., pp. 30–31.
4. Liebe F. Cavalieri, "Genetic Engineering: A Blind Plunge," *The Washington Post,* 14 May 1982.
5. *National Agricultural Lands Study* (Washington, D.C.: U.S. Government Printing Office, 1981). Includes four volumes, with a useful Executive Summary.
6. *The Empty Breadbasket?* A study of the U.S. food system by the Cornucopia Project of Rodale Press (Emmaus, Penn.: Rodale Press, 1981), p. 23. For statistics on the trends of farm ownership, see also the U.S. Department of Agriculture's *A Time to Choose: Summary Report on the Structure of Agriculture* (Washington, D.C.: Government Printing Office, January 1981).
7. Ibid., p. 34.
8. Ibid., p. 36.
9. Ibid., p. 39.
10. "Where Have All the Farmlands Gone?" brochure prepared by the National Agricultural Lands Study (Washington, D.C., 1980).
11. Gerald O. Barney, study director, *The Global 2000 Report to the President: Entering the Twenty-First Century,* 3 vols. (Washington, D.C.: Government Printing Office, 1980). The report consists of three volumes: Volume I: Summary; Volume II: The Technical Report: Volume III: Documentation of the Government's Global Sectoral Models: The Government's "Global Model."
12. Ibid., 1:23.
13. Ibid., 1:26.
14. United Nations Environment Programme, "The State of the World Environment, 1972–1982," report of the executive director, January 29, 1982, p. 28.
15. Quoted in Susan Abbasi, "Review of the Global Environment Ten Years after Stockholm; Summary and Analysis of Hearings" (prepared for the Subcommittee on Human Rights and International Organizations, committee on Foreign Affairs, House of Representatives), Congressional Research Service (6 May 1982), p. 21.
16. *Global 2000,* 1:40.
17. "Running Dry," *Wall Street Journal,* 6 August 1980, p. 2.
18. *Empty Breadbasket?* p. 65.
19. Ibid., p. 69.
20. Ibid., p. 69.
21. "Florida's Battle of the Swamp," *Time,* 24 August 1981, p. 41.
22. *Empty Breadbasket?* p. 71.
23. Ibid., p. 74.
24. *Global 2000,* 2:155.
25. Ibid.
26. "World Environment, 1972–1982," p. 24.
27. *Global 2000,* 2:151.
28. Ibid.

29. David Doniger, "Hold Your Breath, The Diesels are Coming," *Amicus Journal*, Winter 1981, pp. 33–34.
30. *Global 2000*, 1:36.
31. Abbasi, "Review of the Global Environment," p. 14.
32. *Global 2000*, 1:51.
33. Abbasi, "Review of the Global Environment," p. 15.
34. "World Environment, 1972–1982," p. 13.
35. *Global 2000*, 1:36.
36. Abbasi, "Review of the Global Environment," p. 13.
37. Ibid.
38. *Global 2000*, 2:161–178.
39. *Global 2000*, 1:27.
40. *Global 2000*, 2:38.
41. Ibid., 2:181–184.
42. Ibid., 2:364.
43. Ibid., 2:367.
44. Ibid., 2:374.
45. Ibid., 2:367.
46. Ibid., 2:378.
47. Ibid.
48. "World Environment, 1972–1982," pp. 30–31.
49. *Global 2000*, 1:9.
50. Ibid., 1:13.
51. "World Environment, 1972–1982," pp. 33–34.
52. *Global 2000*, 1:39.

2. The Guilt of Christendom

What lies behind the desecration of the world? What has brought humanity to the brink of destroying the life of the creation? Many answer those questions with a stinging indictment: Christianity is to blame.

The famed historian Arnold Toynbee has charged, "The recklessly extravagant consumption of nature's irreplaceable treasures —and the pollution of those of them that man has not already devoured—can be traced back in the last analysis to a religious cause, and . . . this cause is the rise of monotheism."[1] Toynbee argues that "man's greedy impulse to exploit nature used to be held in check by his pious worship of nature. This primitive inhibition has been removed by the rise and spread of monotheism."[2] Genesis 1:28, with its command to "subdue the earth," shattered the inherent respect humanity had for nature. "This injunction to 'subdue,' " argues Toynbee, "which modern man has taken as his directive, is surely immoral, impracticable, and disastrous."[3] Toynbee's proposed remedy is to return to pantheism.

With nostalgia, Toynbee looks to pre-Christian Greek religion, as well as to Confucianism, Taoism, and Shinto, as pantheistic religious traditions that see divinity within nature and focus on harmony with it. Others, such as René Dubos, the noted biologist and author, have described cases of the ruthless exploitation of nature in pre-Christian and non-Christian cultures.[4] Yet, most primitive cultures not rooted in the Western Christian world generally regard nature as having sacred qualities. The people of these cultures see their lives religiously interconnected with the life of the natural world.

Closest to home, traditional native American culture is rooted in a reverential relationship to nature that conflicts sharply with the white, Western, Christian view. Dedicated scholars such as Joseph

Epps Brown, who wrote *The Sacred Pipe,* have attempted to portray freshly the qualities of native American religion to the white
culture.[5]

In my experience, I have learned the most about this tradition
from two friends, Charlie and Elizabeth. He grew up as a white
evangelical and married Elizabeth, who is a member of the Lakota
tribe. We were together in Sojourners Fellowship in Washington
D.C., and they subsequently left to establish their home and raise
their family on the Lakota reservation in South Dakota.

A year later, a letter from Charlie explained his experience of
Lakota spirituality and its view of life, as contrasted with views he
was taught in his evangelical tradition:

When most Christians talk about being good stewards of the earth, what
they have in mind is something like this: We conserve resources so we can
use them in the future, and we conserve some wildlife areas so we can
admire and enjoy their beauty. I don't think this is biblically sound because both of these ideas are still caught up in human idolatry. This type
of stewardship is still human oriented. The creation exists for the welfare
of the human race in this thinking. I don't believe that. I think we all are
part of the entire creation, with our own unique roles, and we exist for
God.

Lakota theology speaks of the great hoop. This great hoop is full of
cycles, which are circles of life. Nature always shows itself to be a series
of cycles or circles. So Lakota people lived in circles (tipis), camped in
circles, viewed human life in circles and their religious ceremonies are
circular in content and ceremony.

When people pray in the sweat lodge they act out the essence of the
universe and its creation. The sweat lodge is like a circular womb. When
you come out of it you've been physically and spiritually purified, or
reborn. It contains the basic elements: air, water, fire, rock/earth. In the
sweat lodge ceremony you pray in the six directions (west, north, east,
south, heaven, and earth) and verbally acknowledge that we all exist
within this circle or sphere, and that at the center of all this is God, or
Wakan Tanka (the Great Mystery, the source of all that is). Everything
begins in God and everything ends in God. The great hoop is complete.

We are all in relationship with one another because we are all in relationship with God. By working with the basic elements in your worship you continually establish your relationship to the rest of creation. And you start thinking in terms of family. The Lakota people have an elaborate kinship system. Included in this relationship system is the earth, who is your grandmother, the sky and eagle, who are your brothers, etc. When you think circular like this you place prime importance on right and proper relationships. You don't abuse or use your relatives, human or otherwise.

White settlers came to America with firmly fixed ideas about land, and the natural resources of this New World. The riches of the continent lie waiting to be exploited; that was the divinely ordained purpose for which these resources had been created, and had now been put at the disposal of Western civilization.

Genocidal treatment was inflicted upon the native Americans not just because of competition for land and resources, but also because of their sharply conflicting ways of relating to the created world. Native Americans, for instance, could not understand how the white man could buy and sell a piece of land, as if it were a mere commodity to be owned.

In the mid-nineteenth century, white settlers near Puget Sound attempted to sign a treaty with a group of Indian tribes, whose lands they had overrun and taken. Chief Sealth, whose name was spelled "Seattle" by the white settlers, had originally welcomed the whites, and even accepted their God, becoming a practicing Christian. Yet, he was deeply fearful of the tragic results stemming from white settlement, both to his people and to the land. In 1854 he delivered a moving address in which he pleaded with the whites to reverse their destruction of the land, the buffalo, and nature's resources:

How can you buy or sell the sky, the warmth of the land? The idea is strange to us. If we do not own the freshness of the air and the sparkle of the water, how can you buy them?

This we know. The earth does not belong to man; man belongs to the earth. This we know. All thing are connected like the blood which unites one family. . . .

Whatever befalls the earth befalls the sons of the earth. Man does not weave the web of life, he is merely a strand in it. Whatever he does to the web, he does to himself.

Chief Seattle went on to talk about the God of the white man and the red man:

You may think now that you own Him as you wish to own our land, but you cannot. He is the God of man and His compassion is equal for the red man and the white. This earth is precious to Him and to harm the earth is to heap contempt on its Creator. Continue to contaminate your bed, and you will one night suffocate in your own waste.

So if we sell you our land, love it as we've loved it. Care for it as we've cared for it. Hold in your mind the memory of the land as it is when you take it. And with all your strength, with all your mind, with all your heart, preserve it for your children and love it . . . as God loves us all.[6]

Chief Seattle's prophetic words were not heeded. And his attempt to appeal to the God of the white and red man as the source for preserving the creation fell on deaf ears and hard hearts. The whites believed their God had given them a harsh land to be subdued and exploited, even ruthlessly. As the U.S. Cavalry swept across the West, chasing, herding and killing Indians like flocks of wild animals, the Christianity brought by the white settlers trampled the native Americans' sense of reverence for the creation.

Historians, philosophers, and environmentalists appear to have the arguments of history on their side when they charge that Christianity is the chief culprit in motivating and justifying the ruin of the earth. Their charges must be taken by Christians with utter seriousness. Like it or not, Christians find themselves on the defensive against a forceful indictment.

The charge against Christianity contains four major points. First, the Genesis 1:28 command for humanity to "have dominion" and "subdue the earth" sets humanity apart from nature and directs humanity to conquer and exploit it. Toynbee's reflections on monotheism are a good example of this argument. Nature is seen merely as a storehouse of raw materials. Those materials have value only as they are exploited and used. A tree, for example, exists to build a house or a ship, or to heat a meal. It becomes valuable as humanity uses it. And humanity's divinely appointed task is to do just that—to place nature firmly under its subjugation.

Nature itself has no sacred qualities and no intrinsic relationship to the Creator. God made nature for humanity to use. In effect, nature is there to do with as humanity pleases. Thus, this perspective is highly anthropocentric. At the center of all creation are human beings; creation exists only for their benefit.

One of the foremost proponents of architecture, design, and land use planning that respects and integrates the inherent values of nature is Ian McHarg. His book *Design with Nature* is a masterful study of how cities and civilization can be constructed cooperatively with nature rather than fighting against it. But in describing the roots of our distorted stance toward nature, McHarg goes back to Genesis:

The affirmation of Jehovah, the God in whose image man was made, was also a declaration of war on nature . . . the Biblical creation story of the first chapter of Genesis, the source of the most generally accepted description of man's role and powers, not only fails to correspond to reality as we observe it, but in its insistence upon dominion and subjugation of nature, encourages the most exploitative and destructive instincts in man rather than those that are deferential and creative. Indeed, if one seeks license for those who would increase radioactivity, create canals and harbors with atomic bombs, employ poisons without constraint, or give consent to the bulldozer mentality, there could be no better injunction than this text.[7]

The second point is that modern science and technology have been enthusiastically blessed by Christianity in their unbridled conquest of nature. Fifteen years ago, a pivotal article by Lynn White, Jr., titled "The Historical Roots of our Ecological Crisis," presented this argument, which quickly found fertile soil among secular environmentalists.[8] The article has been reprinted countless times since then, and has come to be regarded as infallible among ecological critics of Christianity.

White himself has an appreciation for the Christian tradition and is a noted social historian of the Middle Ages. His article presented the now-familiar charge that Christianity condoned a transcendent, exploitative stance toward nature. But the crux of his argument was that Christianity in the West spawned the growth of modern science, which grew out of natural theology. Further, Christian values in the Middle Ages encouraged the development of modern technology, which flourished under a doctrine of humanity's transcendence over nature. These two new forces—science and technology—then merged together with the blessing of Christianity, giving humanity unprecedented and uncontrolled power over nature, and resulting in disasterous ecological consequences. For this, White alleges, "Christianity bears a huge burden of guilt."[9]

Critics of White argue that his thesis does not account for reckless attitudes toward nature evident in various non-Christian cultures, and that he ignores the ways in which the forces of industrialization, urbanization, and the capitalistic drive to increase wealth have caused a large measure of the world's ecological crisis. They see the problem as political and economic, rather than religious. White's response is that the "roots" of the crisis can be traced to Western Christendom's blessing of the methods and tools that have unlocked the modern world's conquest of nature.[10]

The third argument accuses Christianity of promoting a dualism between the spiritual and the material, making the things of this earth of little importance, or even regarding them as evil. The soul is separated from its mortal and decaying body, just as heaven is divorced from an earth corrupted by sin. Nature itself, according to some Christian thought, is shot throughout with sin's deadly corruption. What is holy in life is separate from the world. The material, the earth, and the body—these pass away, and are destroyed. Only the spiritual survives, and is worthy of value. Earth is on hell's side; we must leave it behind spiritually, for its destiny is death.

Why, then, care for the earth (or for the body, for that matter)? In the words of the gospel hymn:

This world is not my home, I'm just a passing through,
My treasures are laid up somewhere beyond the blue.
The angels beckon me from heaven's open door,
and I can't feel at home in this world anymore.

If we are not at home in the world, and are not motivated therefore to improve the earthly setting, then we are justified in escaping from it. Wendell Berry, the perceptive poet and essayist, portrays the effects of this dualism in this way:

The great disaster of human history is one that happened to or within religion: that is, the conceptual division between the holy and the world, the excerpting of the Creator from the Creation. . . . The contempt for the world or the hatred of it, that is exemplified both by the wish to exploit it for the sake of cash and by the willingness to despise it for the sake of "salvation," has reached a terrifying climax in our own time. The rift between soul and body, the Creator and the Creation, has admitted the entrance into the world of the machinery of the world's doom.[11]

The division between the spiritual and the material is deepened by a hierarchical interpretation of the creation account in Genesis. God is up at the top, and beneath him are men; beneath them are women, and children. Beneath them are the animals; lower than them are the plants, and then the inanimate parts of the created world. God is the ultimate Good, and each step down from Him becomes more inferior. Just as God is to rule over man, men are to rule over women. Mankind (with the emphasis on man) is to subdue the world of nature.[12]

The same biblical interpretation that attempts to justify female subordination to males sanctions humanity to subjugate nature. And while nature has frequently been given feminine qualities, so that we even speak of nature as "mother" and read the *Mother Earth News,* man's ruthless exploitation of nature becomes the "rape of the earth." On the other hand, those arriving at a feminist interpretation of Scripture can offer a theology that not only frees females from male domination, but also treats nature as a subject for cooperation rather than an object of conquest.[13]

The fourth and last point in the charge against Christianity is that the belief in the Second Coming, which will usher in God's total reign, negates any reason to improve or even preserve the world until then. In a fashion that has gained wide popularity, some Christians argue that we must expect the world to get worse. All these events, including the depletion of resources and the devastation of the world's ecological balance, simply indicate that Christ's coming is closer at hand. Trying to prevent such happenings is both fruitless and pointless.

Evangelical authors such as Hal Lindsey in *The Late Great Planet Earth* have given wide currency to these views. Theologically, they believe in "dispensational premillennialism." This teaches that after Christ's Second Coming, a kingdom will be set up by him on earth for 1,000 years. Peace will reign, and the world of nature will also exhibit a new peace, harmony, and fruitfulness. Biblical passages referring to such hopes apply only to this millennial kingdom.

According to this view, to attempt to change humanity's relationship to the creation now is hopeless. We should expect a downward spiral of ruin and catastrophe. All this will be dramatically changed only by Christ's return. Understandably, writers like Anthony Ette and Robert Waller, in their *Ecologist Quarterly* article "The Anomaly of a Christian Ecology," argue that "the doctrine of the Second coming has . . . militated against ecological living as it teaches that this world is ephemeral and hence unimportant."[14]

More shocking, however, was to hear similar views expressed positively by evangelical James Watt, President Reagan's first Interior Secretary. When asked by the House Interior Committee about his views on conserving resources for future generations, Watt replied, "I do not know how many future generations we can count on before the Lord returns."[15] Such statements by James Watt simply confirmed the worst fears of environmentalists about the stance of Christians toward the resources of creation.

Is Christianity guilty as charged? Can the blame for the destruction of creation's resources be laid at the trampling feet of the church? Does biblical faith offer any redeeming vision to guide modern humanity's precarious relationship to the creation? Can the church demonstrate any alternative paths for the preservation and sustaining of this world's life? These are the questions we will explore together in the next chapters of this book.

John Black, in *The Dominion of Man*, perceptively summarizes the challenge we face:

> Dominion over his environment has proceeded so far as to encourage man to arrogate to himself the role of its creator. If Christianity will be shown in the end to have failed the world, it will have failed because it encouraged man to set himself apart from nature, or, at the very least, because it failed to discourage him from doing this . . . The end result of dissociating himself from the rest of nature has been to dissociate himself also from the belief in a divine creator.[16]

Can Christianity save the world? Many doubt it. And countless Christians haven't thought about it. The church faces the urgent task today of first asking, and then attempting to answer, that question honestly and biblically. The stakes are high, even ultimate. For in the midst of creation's contemporary crisis, which each day makes the world's future look more bleak and dim, humanity is asking whether there is a Creator whose life can be trusted for the salvation of this world.

NOTES

1. Arnold Toynbee, "The Religious Background of the Present Environmental Crisis," in *Ecology and Religion in History*, David and Eileen Spring (New York: Harper & Row, 1974), p. 146.
2. Ibid., p. 145.
3. Ibid., p. 149.
4. René Dubos, "A Theology of the Earth," *Western Man and Environmental Ethics*, ed. Ian Barbour (Reading, Mass.: Addison-Wesley, 1973), pp. 43–54.
5. Joseph Epps Brown, *The Sacred Pipe: The Seven Rites of the Oglala Sioux* (Norman, Okla.: University of Oklahoma Press, 1953). There are several fine works concerning native American religion comprising a whole separate bibliography. Joseph Epps Brown's *The Sacred Pipe* grew out of time Brown spent living with Black Elk, a holy man of the Oglala Sioux, in 1947. John Neihardt's *Black Elk Speaks* (Lincoln: University of Nebraska Press, 1961) had previously revealed the vision of this remarkable man to the white culture. In *Seeing with a Native Eye*, ed. Walter Holden Capps (New York: Harper & Row, 1976), Joseph Epps Brown and others offer helpful insights. Two other works serving as an introduction to the subject are Sam D. Gill's *Native Ameri-*

can Religions (Belmont, Calif.: Wadsworth Publishing Company, 1982) and *Teachings from the American Earth,* ed. Dennis and Barbara Tedlock (New York: Liveright, 1975).

6. John M. Rich, *Chief Seattle's Unanswered Challenge* (Seattle: Lowman and Hanford, 1947).

7. Ian McHaig, *Design with Nature* (Garden City, New York: The National History Press, 1969), p. 26.

8. Lynn White, Jr., "The Historical Roots of our Ecological Crisis," *Western Man and Environmental Ethics,* pp. 18–30. This is only one of numerous books in which White's essay appears. But this volume includes responses to White, and White's response to his critics.

9. Ibid., p. 27.

10. Ibid., pp. 55–65.

11. Wendell Berry, "A Secular Pilgrimage," *Western Man and Environmental Ethics,* p. 135.

12. A very forceful presentation of this position is found in Elizabeth Dobson Gray, *Green Paradise Lost* (Wellesley, Mass.: Roundtable Press, 1979).

13. See, for example, Rosemary Ruether, *New Woman, New Earth* (New York: Seabury Press, 1975).

14. Anthony Ette and Robert Waller, "The Anomaly of a Christian Ecology," *Ecologist Quarterly,* Summer 1978, pp. 144–148.

15. Colman McCarthy, "James Watt and the Puritan Ethic," *The Washington Post,* 14 May 1981.

16. John Black, *The Dominion of Man* (Edinburgh: Edinburgh University Press, 1970) p. 121.

3. The Conquest of Nature

A drive through the suburban streets of any large American city reveals clues to modern humanity's relationship to nature. The streets in the suburb where I grew up have names like Greenwood, Belle Plaines ("beautiful plains"), Vine, and Chestnut. The suburbs are called Brookfield, Western Springs, Elmhurst, and Des Plaines ("the plains"). The first shopping center I remember in the Chicago suburbs was called Old Orchard. It has been succeeded by Oak Brook and Woodfield. The names of these streets, cities, and shopping malls refer to the natural settings they have destroyed.

Today we pay pallid tribute to these natural settings, which have been systematically bulldozed and removed from our midst. The modern urbanized American is reminded of this displaced nature chiefly by street signs, billboards, and television. Advertising seizes on images of a lost intimacy with nature to sell us the products of a consumer society that has spawned so much injury to the earth. Native Americans sell us Mazola Corn Oil, naturally. We are beckoned to come to Marlboro country. Country freshness can be enjoyed year 'round, "because you can't take the country out of Salem," and J & B Scotch "whispers" across the lonely, mist-covered mountain lakes on our magazine pages.

Nature has become a place where you can go, either in your mind's eye or in person. Nature trails offer a brief excursion into this lost garden. Thousands drive to national parks in order to "see nature," which is reduced to a tourist attraction. Tropical islands, despite how much they are cluttered with tourist hotels, are advertised as having virgin beaches. Nature is an interlude—one enters it for a while, pauses, and then returns from it.

For the modern technician, business person, or scientist, nature has become a raw reservoir of material to be studied, manipulated, and exploited. The theme is domination. The workings of nature must be objectively analyzed and understood. The raw materials of nature must be extracted and utilized, and the forces of nature must be controlled, harnessed, and manipulated.

We sentimentalize nature on the one hand and dominate it on the other, and we take these relationships more or less for granted, rarely suspecting that other alternatives exist, or have any practical relevance.

But the modern view of nature is an aberration. Humanity has not always had such a peculiar attitude towards its natural environment—plundering it in fact while extolling its grandeur for commercial purposes. Much of the nonindustrialized world knows little of this relationship even today.

The forces of modern life have decisively altered our relationship to nature. Of all the changes introduced to civilization by the rise of the modern world since the Enlightenment and the Industrial Revolution, perhaps none is so profound and so unconscious as the new relationship humanity bears to nature.

What has happened? What forces have brought about this change? What are its consequences?

The change in humanity's relationship to creation is linked to humanity's changing understanding of how God is related to nature. The modern world has secularized nature. Either as raw material or as an object of sentiment, nature exists as a thing unto itself, without any connection to God.

Secularization occurs when our understanding of the world and its structures is no longer based on religious assumptions. One helpful definition of this process is given by Charles West: "Secularism is the withdrawal of areas of thought and life from religious—and finally also from metaphysical—control, and the attempt to understand and live in in these areas in the terms which they alone offer."[1] By detaching God from nature and regarding it as secular, humanity has changed the terms of its relationship to nature.

Rather than a subject to which we are related, nature has become an object from which we are detached. Nature is something "out there," apart from us and apart from God. This detachment enables first of all objective study, and then manipulation and control. Domination and exploitation of this external material of nature can be undertaken without any religious restraints. Meanwhile, a superficial and nostalgic picture of nature is fostered by advertising images and preserved in wilderness areas and wildlife preserves.

Some theologians view the impact of modern science and technology on the earth as being an entirely liberating step forward, and one that will make human life more livable. They compliment Christianity for these achievements and welcome the process of secularization as Christianity's gift to the world.[2] Rather than remaining imprisoned in narrow and archaic superstitions and keeping people in fear and bondage, they say, Christianity—through its myth-defying force of secularization—frees humanity from these inhibitions in order to embrace a creative role in the world and build humanity's new destiny. Harvey Cox's famous *The Secular City,* for example, supports such secularization.[3]

Today, such theologies of secularization have lost their appeal, largely because the modern world's dearth of moral discernment and vision has become painfully obvious. It hardly seems adequate to describe the gospel's contribution to the modern world in terms of the forces of modern secularism that emanate from a transcendent God who relativizes, judges, and liberates humanity from unmodern religion.

The more common argument heard today is that modern humanity's exploitative view of nature has its roots in Genesis. The transcendent God of Judeo-Christianity destroyed the sense of sacredness within nature, writing the Magna Carta for the conquest of nature by science and technology—an argument summarized in the last chapter. Whether one curses the consequences of this divinely ordained conquest of nature or blesses the technological fruits of modern secularism, the underlying assumption is that biblical faith gave rise to these historical developments. But is that true?

What is the relationship between Christian tradition and the reign of modern science and technology? Was it one verse in Genesis that overturned humanity's traditional relationship to nature? Is it historically true to allege that the modern impulse that reduced nature to a quantifiable, desacralized object to be dominated by humanity was engendered by biblical revelation?

Obviously volumes can be written—and have been—exploring these questions. But one cogent piece, "Man and Nature: The Ecological Controversy and the Old Testament," written by Old Testament scholar James Barr, can serve as a useful example.[4] Barr argues that "the whole connection set up between the Bible and modern science and technology is thoroughly faulty and needs to be entirely rethought."[5]

Barr rejects the argument that humanity being created "in the image of God" implies that humanity has "dominion" over nature. Further, he maintains that to "have dominion" and "subdue the earth," as spoken of in Genesis 1:26–8, does not place the emphasis on "man's power or on his exploitative activities"[6] (we will examine interpretations of these scriptures more closely in the next chapter). In addition, Barr asks that if the Hebrews did have unique cultural insights regarding science and technology, would they not have produced something distinctive in their lives along these lines? But neither the Bible nor archeology has produced the evidence for anything remarkable and unique in Hebrew technology. Finally, Barr doubts that the myths and religions surrounding Hebrew culture were distinguished primarily by their sense of nature worship. And even where that was the case, Barr observes, "it is not clear that cultures which had advanced nature-religions or advanced mythologies were thereby necessarily inhibited from making remarkable technological advances."[7] A dramatic case in point is the ancient Egyptians' building of the pyramids. Nature religions didn't prevent techological development, nor did transcendent religion spawn such accomplishments.

Of course, biblical texts such as Genesis 1:28 have been used to justify and rationalize an exploitative view toward nature. But the fact that such an attitude can find a biblical text that seems to condone it in no way demonstrates that the Bible caused humanity to change its relationship to nature. It only proves that people like to use the Bible to justify their opinions and actions.

Looking at history, then, we find that it is inappropriate to hold the Bible responsible for modern humanity's dramatically changed relationship to nature. Granted, modern science and technology arose in the Western world, which was penetrated with certain Christian interpretations of life. And the growth of science and technology interacted in a variety of ways, some positive and some negative, with the Christian tradition in its Western form. But we need to look elsewhere to discover the roots of modern humanity's relationship to nature.[8]

The answer, in my judgment, is found largely in understanding the impact of the Enlightenment and the scientific revolution on how we all think about, and relate to, nature. The secularization of nature has its roots not in the Bible, but in the evolution of modern thinking, according to which humanity removed itself from nature in order to objectively observe, understand, and ultimately control it.

When Francis Bacon developed what we understand today as the scientific method, he did much to help enshrine this new relationship between humanity and nature. Bacon's conviction, as described by one author using Bacon's own words, was that "nature must be 'bound into service' and made a 'slave,' put 'in constraint' and 'molded' by the mechanical arts. The 'searchers and spies of nature' are to discover her plots and secrets."[9] Nature was to be enslaved by man, therefore; it was to yield both knowledge and power. "By art and the hand of man," Bacon wrote, nature can be "forced out of her natural state and squeezed and molded." The result is that "human knowledge and human power meet as one."[10]

Other key figures contributed to this revolution in thought and practice. Galileo, defending the ideas of Copernicus, asserted that a true knowledge of nature could be gained through grasping its mathematical laws. He was tried by the church not simply for his contention that the earth revolved around the sun, but also for his insistence that this was *truth*—a fact verifiable by the laws of the universe, and not just a hypothesis.

Descartes detached the human mind from nature: A person's body was a machine, like that of any other animal, except that it had a mind, and an ability to think. Newton explained the laws of motion in the universe in mathematical terms.[11] Thus mechanical models of the universe as a clock whose workings could be understood through rigorous examination and a knowledge of mathematical laws seemed persuasive. God was the one who had simply wound the clock up and then stepped aside. This mechanical paradigm of the world excluded God as the explanation of and force within the functioning of the world.

Developed further, this way of thinking about the world led to an entrenched materialist view of reality. At its core, what the world consisted of were particles, arranged in various ways and functioning according to certain mathematical laws, which made the objects—some with life and some without—that we see, observe, and interact with.

Once Bacon, Descartes, Newton, and others liberated God from running the natural world, John Locke set God free from the task of upholding government and society. Natural reason and self-interest would suffice. This philosophy was heartily condoned and blessed by Adam Smith in constructing an economics without God.

The views of Locke and Smith helped give political and economic expression to this changing relationship toward nature. The resources of nature were seen as a massive and inexhaustible storehouse of raw materials waiting to be exploited by humanity and thus transformed into beneficial use. Nature's resources, then, were given value only as they were useful, through technology's application of science. These views undergirded a vision of new political freedom and economic plentitude. As a new world of untouched resources was being discovered, and as the Industrial Revolution unfolded, that vision seemed to have history on its side.

Philosophers still struggled to identify a proper domain for God, principally in humanity's hopes, desires, and historical destiny. Feuerbach, however, removed those from God, claiming they were mere projections, and Marx proceeded logically with an agenda of history and destiny dependent upon humanity's "reality" rather than its illusions.

Regarding humanity's relationship to nature, however, Marx accepted the stance of Smith, Locke, and others shaping the modern mind. According to Marx, nature was a reservoir of raw resources, and nothing more, which were to be transformed through the building of industrialized society. The crucial difference was that the working class would control the process and thus share in the fruits of this transformation by owning the means of production.[12]

Darwin, a contemporary of Marx, removed God from creation itself. The immediate popularity of his ideas was due in large part to the evolving desire of the modern mind to answer the question of ultimate origin nontheistically. A last refuge for God was sought in the human psyche—in feelings, emotions, and inner self. But Freud banished God from that domain.

Thus the modern mindset, in its understanding of the world, of nature, of reality, of history, and of self, has peeled away the assumption of God's existence, or God's relationship to anything that matters.

This is not to suggest that the contributions of such seminal thinkers lack any truth, validity, or value. Those contributions are evident and need not be disputed. But we must be honest in saying that the modern mind, as it has developed over the past few centuries, has constructed a view of reality, nature, and life as if God did not exist.[13]

Jeremy Rifkin writes, "Concepts of nature do not so much reveal nature as they do our compulsive desire to escape from its clutches."[14] Certainly this was true of the materialistic mechanical model of nature emerging from the scientific revolution. Today, of course, modern physics repudiates such a view. Scientists from many fields question the adequacy of the model of nature bequeathed to us by the pioneers of the scientific revolution.[15] Yet, the modern world has a firm determination to understand and treat nature as a secular object.

We tend to think that enlightened minds merely discarded the belief in God as a practical matter, for it no longer seemed necessary. But that view is far too simple and culture-bound. What changed fundamentally was humanity's relationship to the world.

The medieval mind assumed that the beings and objects in the world possessed another reality, one that could not be perceived, but a reality to which the observer was also related. Perceiving phenomena involved participation in them. This accounts for the easy interplay of the "real" and the supernatural in medieval painting. A quote by Owen Barfield may be helpful here:

It is clear that [medieval man] did not feel himself isolated by his skin from the world outside him to quite the same extent that we do. He was integrated or mortised into it, each different part of him being united to a different part of it by some invisible thread. In his relation to his environment, the man of the middle ages was rather less like an island, rather more like an embryo than we are.[16]

This was radically changed by the scientific revolution. The self began to be perceived as separate from the world, and the world was perceived as the sum total of particles that could be observed, analyzed, and controlled. The intrinsic participation of the person in observed phenomena was simply denied, and the world "out there" was externalized, objectified, and secularized.

Another important transition occurred in the development of our contemporary view of nature. The theories and hypotheses about the external world's composition and functioning came to be regarded as facts, as actual descriptions of what was real. Previously, when phenomena were understood to represent a separate, unobservable reality, it was impossible to relate to the phenomena themselves as final reality, or to know in fact the actual workings of the world simply through observing or studying the phenomena in and of themselves. Hypotheses were truly just that.

But if ultimately only particles are real, then the theories and hypotheses about them are regarded as truth.

With this mindset, then, the modern mind looks back through history, regarding past cultures (or present "primitive" cultures) as simply possessing wrongheaded ideas about the world—unenlightened ones—rather than recognizing the vastly changed relationship between the person and the world. Against the backdrop of this mindset, modern theology has attempted to perform its task, making God understandable on a seemingly godless stage.

Given this understanding of the evolution in modern thought, critics like Lynn White, Jr., are suddenly thrown into a different light. It was not Christianity that instituted the division of humanity from nature, giving impetus to the free reign of technology over nature, with its lamentable results. This division was the consequence of the modern mind freeing itself from a religious perspective and setting out to manipulate and control nature and the world.

It was these forces that distorted a Christian understanding of the world and rendered biblical faith impotent as the guardian of the natural world and its relationship to humanity.

Asserting, as White did, that "to a Christian, a tree can be no more than a physical fact" is a gross misunderstanding. That is what a tree is according to the modern *scientific* view. And if a Christian accepts a tree as merely a physical phenomenon, it only reveals how deeply the modern mind has seduced Christian thinking.

White and others are right in underscoring Christianity's rejection of animism. The tree is not a god. But modern thinking, rather than biblical faith, concludes from this that the tree is only a physical fact.

Yet, contemporary Christian theology has had very little to say about what the tree is, or what its relationship to ourselves and to God might be. Why has it been so ineffectual in this area? What accounts for its silence? And why has it so easily been a pawn used to justify the modern treatment of nature?

Faced with the pressure of modern thought to eliminate God as the starting point, theology has been largely reactive. Fundamentalism drew the battle line between the Bible and Darwin. The result was that Darwin became regarded as inspired, if not inerrant, by all who were not fundamentalists.

Those who believed in the Bible found little success in challenging the modern world view and gradually lost interest in conclusively refuting it. Rather, their faith was known and experienced in almost exclusively personal terms. God saved them from the world. Worldly came to mean sinful. Society around them seemed hostile to fundamentalist Christianity, and they took refuge in God's judgment of the world and God's salvation of their souls.

Though this stance, of course, was not unique in the church's history, its adaptation to the modern age has had a striking influence on fundamentalist and evangelical ways of thinking. A radical separation between the material and the spiritual fractured the world view of many Bible-believing Christians. And, naturally, they read this distortion back into the Bible.

The modern age declared that reality was only matter, and that only it mattered. Evangelicals, in response, decided that if matter was only matter, then it didn't matter. Once the scientific modern view had emptied the world of God, fundamentalist Christian faith saw little reason to save the world. It fought hard for a time to save presumably biblical beliefs about the world, but that was (and still is) only a fight to salvage their ideas.

Liberal Christianity did want to save the world, while at the same time trying to accommodate Christian belief to what the modern age was declaring as fact and truth. Its objective was to locate God in the evolutionary progress of human history. The gospel became social, rather than "other-wordly." Faith in God became faith in the ability of the social order to evolve into the Kingdom of God. But as the twentieth century unfolded, those tenets became increasingly suspect and dubious.

Karl Barth then entered the scene with a theology of crisis and the word that shattered liberal Protestantism and dramatically shaped the contours of contemporary Christian thought.

Barth asserted that the initiative in Christian faith is always with God and not with humanity. God reveals, God addresses, God acts, God saves. This initiative of grace judges, humbles, and devastates humanity's idolatrous attempts to know God, please God, or be like God. The Word of God addresses humanity over-against human culture, history, and activity. It is received at the point of crisis, as one realizes the existential absurdity of human life, which is the final nihilistic outcome of the modern mindset.

Barth stressed that the contemporary age—indeed, any age—cannot know God through reason, through the observation of the natural world, or through a faith in the progress of history. He decisively rejected natural theology—the view that humanity's reason, applied to understanding the natural order, leads to a knowledge of God. This building-block theory of knowing God in the world through rationality, in the natural order, in the works of humanity, in culture, and in historical progress all seemed to Barth as a central obstacle to true faith in God. God transcends us and the world; God is beyond our human ability to reach, control, and manipulate; God comes to us through saving grace.

This stance was critical when applied by Barth to the state, politics, and culture. Attempts to see God's spirit expressed in a given culture and to use God for sanctifying a state's political order was utter idolatry, in Barth's view, and fraught with the most terrible consequences. Barth and his followers witnessed this in the rise of National Socialism in Germany, and formulated the Barmen Confession and the Confessing Church in response.

Barth and his followers accentuated God's separation from the world of nature. Barthian theology, to use his term, is "the-anthropological." This means it focuses on the "doctrine of communion and fellowship between *God and man.*"[17] Paul Santmire, the theologian who has studied Barth perhaps the most thoroughly on this point, writes:

In his doctrine of creation, Barth states emphatically that theology here had to do only with God and man! It knows nothing, says Barth, of any relationship betwen God and nature. . . . Although there are many complexities in Barth's doctrine of God and in his anthropology, the end result of his arduous thirteen-volume argumentation, as far as our interests are concerned, is the reaffirmation of an exclusively the-anthropological, essentially unecological theology. Nature for Barth is merely a stage.[18]

Despite its very significant contribution to contemporary Christian thought, Barthian theology focuses only on God's relationship to humanity. Therein lies its inability to respond to the crisis facing the world of creation; in its fervency to reject natural theology, it also deprives the Christian of any sound basis for constructing a theology of nature.

Some recent theologians have attempted to develop patterns of Christian thought that build upon a more connected view of the relationship between God, humanity, and nature. Many of these, classified as "process theologians," have been influenced by the philosopher Alfred North Whitehead;[19] and the theology of Teilhard de Chardin, the Catholic paleontologist-turned-theologian, attempted to integrate an evolutionary view of the universe into a vision of cosmic fulfillment in Christ. But objections to each have relegated such thought to the periphery of modern theology. Santmire summarized the situation, especially within Protestantism, well:

For the most part, ecologically speaking, the exclusively the-anthropological theology represented by Barth has carried the day within mainstream Protestant thought . . . modern Protestantism has, by and large, become ecologically bankrupt.[20]

I remember how these realizations first struck me at a small gathering of evangelicals, a meeting of which the purpose was to discuss the ecological crisis. Like many classified by the media as "radical evangelicals," I had been deeply influenced by streams of Barthian thought, particularly concerning the Christian's relationship to culture, to the state, and to politics. Theologians like Jacques Ellul, William Stringfellow, and John Howard Yoder—all of whom resonate with Barth on such issues—had been my own mentors.

The evangelical awakening to issues of social and political concern evolved largely in reaction to the Vietnam War and Watergate. Those events shocked many evangelicals into rethinking their relationship to American culture and to our political system. The politics of Jesus was rediscovered and applied. Siding with the poor, opposing war and violence, combatting economic injustice, and confronting the powers that be were found to be just as biblical as the Virgin Birth. Thus social and political questions regarding God's relationship to humanity, and the confrontation of the gospel with the political and economic systems of the world, have been in the center of attention.

Faced with the barbarous, self-righteous slaughter in Vietnam, which was condoned and even blessed by an evangelical church so thoroughly accommodated to the U.S. society, recovering the gospel's "over-againstness" to the culture and the pretensions of the state was, and still is, imperative. But the theology that has been most helpful to me and many others on these pressing social and political concerns seems seriously handicapped in dealing with the danger of ecological catastrophe.

Faced with threats to earth, water, air, and fire, the very fabric of life, another theological approach and new ways to understand the biblical message seem to be required.

Our starting point is to recognize how modern culture has secularized nature and enshrined a destructive relationship between humanity and nature as the norm:

The great modern exploitation of nature has taken place under the reign of a liberal humanism in which man no longer conceives of himself as being under a creator, and in which therefore his place of dominance in the universe and his right to dispose of nature for his own ends is, unlike the situation in the Bible, unlimited.[21]

NOTES

1. James C. Logan, "The Secularization of Nature," in *Christians and the Good Earth* (Alexandria, Va.: The Faith–Man–Nature Group, n.d.), p. 101.
2. See, for example, how this position is summarized and then refuted in "Creation and Environment" by John MacQuarrie, in *Ecology and Religion in History* (New York: Harper & Row, 1974), pp. 32–47. Also, James Logan in "The Secularization of Nature" discusses in particular the influence of Friedrich Gogarten in developing a theology of secularization. "The key . . . is to be found in the concept of 'desacralization' " (p. 106).
3. Harvey Cox, "Creation and Environment," in *The Secular City* (New York: Macmillan, 1965). MacQuarrie characterizes Cox's theology in this manner. This point is discussed briefly in reference to Cox and various theologians by Jack Rogers in "Ecological Theology: The Search for an Appropriate Model," in *Septuagesimo Anno* (Uitgeversmaatschappij J. H. Kok Kampen, 1973), pp. 181–199.
4. James Barr, "The Ecological Controversy and the Old Testament," in *Ecology and Religion in History*, pp. 48–75.
5. Ibid., p. 59.

6. Ibid., p. 61.

7. Ibid., p. 72.

8. This leaves open the discussion of the historical roots of modern science and technology, a subject far beyond the scope of this volume and the competence of this author. But a few notes can be mentioned. In the article cited, James Barr suggests that Greek science, despite its significant differences in understanding, is the earliest foundation for the development of modern science and technology. Clarence Glacken's monumental work, *Traces on the Rhodian Shore: Nature and Culture in Western Thought from Ancient Times to the End of the Eighteenth Century* (Berkeley: University of California Press, 1967), demonstrates that the idea of man's control over nature is present in certain streams of early Greek thought. William Leiss's *The Domination of Nature* (New York: Braziller, 1972) argues that the idea of humanity's lordship over nature stemmed out of biblical roots but was modified by humanity's accountability to God. The rise of modern science and technology became identified with this idea of mastery over nature, and the restraining ethic of accountability to God gradually dissolved. The result was an uninhibited extension of raw "power" over nature, particularly by one sector of society over another.

9. Carolyn Merchant, *The Death of Nature* (San Francisco: Harper & Row, 1980), p. 169.

10. Ibid., p. 171.

11. These assertions are, of course, vast generalizations, summarizing the complex thinking of major intellectuals in just a few sentences. Despite this limitation, however, I think the essential points are valid.

12. A strong statement of this perspective on Marx can be found by American Indian leader Russell Means in "Fighting Words on the Future of the Earth," *Mother Jones,* December 1980, pp. 24–38. William Leiss in *Domination of Nature* offers a differing view of Marx, stressing that what we call domination of nature is actually the domination of one class over another.

13. A brilliant and comprehensive summary of these thinkers, and one that was very helpful to me, is found in Hans Küng, *Does God Exist?* (Garden City, N.Y.: Doubleday and Company, 1980).

14. Jeremy Rifkin, *Algeny* (New York: Viking Press, 1983). From prepublication galley.

15. Again, this statement requires nearly a separate bibliography. But for one example of how the traditional model of nature is being questioned at the level of biology, see Rupert Sheldrake, *A New Science of Life* (Los Angeles: J. P. Tarcher, 1982).

16. Owen Barfield, *Saving the Appearances* (New York: Harcourt Brace Jovanovich, n.d.), p. 78.

17. H. Paul Santmire, "Reflections on the Alleged Ecological Bankruptcy of Western Theology" in *Ethics for Environment: Three Religious Strategies,* ed. Steffenson, Herrscher, and Cook (Green Bay, Wisc.: UWGB Ecumenical Center, 1973), p. 30.

18. Ibid., pp. 30–31.

19. Several important thinkers could be noted here, but perhaps the clearest and most important is John B. Cobb, *Is It Too Late?* (Beverly Hills, Calif.: Benziger Bruce and Glencoe, Inc., 1972). Others include Norman Pittenger and Charles Hartshorne.

20. Santmire, "Ecological Bankruptcy," p. 31.

21. Barr, "Ecological Controversy," p. 73.

II. THE PROMISE: CREATION REDEEMED

4. Subdue the Earth?

Our culture's understanding of nature is thoroughly pagan. To modern culture, nature is the raw, living stuff of the world—the trees, mountains, grass, sea, and animals. This "world of nature" has a separate existence, apart from humanity and apart from God.

The word "nature," as commonly understood in modern society, does not even appear in the Bible. That indicates how foreign our concept of nature is to biblical thinking. The Hebrew language has no word to equal what we understand as "nature" because the idea didn't exist in their thinking and experience.

To the Old Testament writers, all the world is God's creation, and its continuing life and preservation are thoroughly dependent upon God. Human and nonhuman life are not easily divided into separate categories; the Old Testament does not commonly speak about humanity *and* the world of nature. Rather, the biblical word is "creation." The given connection between humanity's livelihood and what we call "nature" is known and assumed.

Our culture assumes a cleavage between humanity and nature. The Bible assumes that both are part of one whole, called the creation. Humanity, of course, has a special and distinct significance in that creation—but in no way does this sever its inherent relationship to the rest of creation.

Likewise, this creation does not exist unto itself, as a separate, autonomous realm. Rather, its life is a continual endowment from the Creator. In the Bible, the life of the world is understandable only in relationship to the life of God. This is the starting point.

The modern view of "nature" is that this autonomous realm has a self-sufficient existence—that there is nothing beyond nature itself. The word "creation," on the other hand, implies that nature is dependent upon the Creator.[1]

Orthodox theologian Paulos Gregorios, in *The Human Presence,* identifies well the non-Christian roots of modern society's view of nature:

The concept of nature as the nonhuman part of the Universe is primarily Indo-Hellenic in origin and becomes particularly prominent in an alienated society, that is, one which has lost its direct sense of dependence on and derivation from God.[2]

In our modern view, we take both our own life, and the life of the world, for granted. Our lives are our own to live, and the material of the world is at our disposal. Sufficient provision of food and shelter is a given in most of our lives. Consumer societies offer countless choices in terms of the abundance of the world's resources, and our assumption is that those choices are ours alone to make.

By contrast, the Old Testament holds the life of creation to be a gift from the Creator. It is a sign of God's blessing that the creation can supply what is necessary to sustain human life. But even that statement is far too narrow and human-centered in its perspective. Biblical writers marvel at how the Creator sustains and preserves the life of all the creation, as, for example, in Psalm 104.

Thus the Bible presents a set of assumptions about the created world that are wholly different than those of our own culture. Further, in its writings about the creation, the Bible poses and answers questions different from those that the church has been asking in recent history.

The modern mind, anxious to explain the universe in a scientifically intelligent manner, has naturally asked how the world, and how humanity, came to be. The questions developed a contemporary relevance for humanity, for in unlocking the secrets of how nature functioned, it was logical to wonder how it began to function that way. And the "how" meant a scientific explanation of causes and effects.

Once Darwin proposed his answers to the "how" of humanity's creation, the church sensed that the truth of the Bible was directly threatened. The defense against Darwin focused on Genesis 1–3 as the Christian explanation of "how" the world came to be. And for many Christians today, this continues to be a chief concern.[3] Pastors about to be ordained in some denominations and regions are asked a question that goes something like this: "If there had been a videotape machine in the Garden of Eden, what would it have recorded?" Such Christians assume that the truth of Genesis 1–3 is equated to its accurate description of literal history.

On the other hand, many Christians who conclude that the first chapters of Genesis are not historical accounts of how the world and humanity originated often dismiss those portions of the Bible as being marginal in their contribution to theology. But in both instances, the truth and value of these chapters is made dependent upon a modern idea that reduces truth to merely scientifically observable or verifiable facts and explanations.

Bringing Genesis into competition with junior high text books on biology in a battle for supposed validity has obscured the deep truths these marvelous chapters of the Bible have to teach us. And this battle has contributed to a general neglect in past years of theology dealing with the creation.[4]

The writers of the Bible were not preoccupied with our modern questions of explaining how, mechanically, the world and human life came into being. They were, however, consistently concerned with the purpose of God in fashioning the creation. As Old Testament scholar Walter Brueggemann points out in his moving commentary on Genesis 1:

> What we have in the text is *proclamation*. The poem does not narrate "how it happened," as though Israel were interested in the *method* of how the world became God's world. Such a way of treating the grand theme of creation is like reducing the marvel of any moving artistic experience to explorations in technique. Israel is concerned with *God's lordly intent,* not his *technique*. . . . It is *news* about a transaction which redefines the world.[5] (Italics his.)

In addition, biblical writers seek to understand the roots of the troubled relationship between God and God's creation. Resistance to God's purpose is evident in creation, but persistence in God's will remains clear. Certain biblical passages about the origin of

God's creation (notably Genesis 2:4–4:16) seek to address this issue.

And then, biblical writers look to the creation—both to its origin and its continuing life—as bearing the glory of God. This sense is enriched by the Old Testament's understanding of the physical life within all the creation, which is evident in many scriptures.[6] As one writer puts it, "Earth itself is alive. . . . The earth has its nature, which makes itself felt and demands respect."[7] Psalm 19:1 is a good example of creation viewed in this perspective: "The heavens are telling the glory of God, and the firmament proclaims his handiwork." The Old Testament proclaims that a primary purpose of creation is to show forth God's glory,[8] and this theme is carried into the New Testament. The view of the created world underlying the Genesis account, and other references as well, is aptly summarized as follows: "Nature is alive through and through, and therefore the more capable of sympathy with man, and of response to the rule of its Creator and Upholder, on whom it directly depends."[9]

In approaching the Bible with concerns about the creation, we not only fail to understand the questions the Bible seeks to answer; we also fail to notice all those places where those questions are addressed. Typically, our focus falls only on the first three chapters of Genesis, so missing the crucial contributions of Genesis 4–11, which in many ways complete the framework begun in Genesis 1–3. Moreover, this narrow focus neglects the many other references in both the Old and New Testaments that deal with creation's origin and purpose.

Several Psalms, including Psalms 8, 19, 74, and 104, are concerned with this theme as well as passages from Jeremiah (27:5 and 32:17) and Isaiah (40:12–31, 45:9–13, 48:12–13). These later passages tie creation to God's redemptive purposes. And books termed the wisdom literature of the Old Testament speak of God's creation of the world through what is called God's "wisdom" (Proverbs 3:19–20, 8:22–31). Further, Job is confronted with a picture of God the Creator in chapters 38–39.

The role of wisdom in the creation's beginning and purpose is further amplified by the New Testament's most powerful text concerning creation, John 1:1–5. Affirmations that the creation came into being through God's Word are made elsewhere as well, such as Hebrews 11:3. Declarations of God as the maker of heaven and earth are repeated frequently in the New Testament (for example, Acts 4:24, 14:15, and 17:24). The origin of all creation in Christ and its unity through Christ find expression in such passages such as 1 Corinthians 8:6, Ephesians 1:10, and in the moving, sweeping passage of Colossians 1:15–17.

We will explore New Testament passages concerning creation in Chapter 6 as well as the familiar Genesis passages shortly, but first let us consider the view of creation found in Psalm 104.

Considered one of the "creation" Psalms, Psalm 104 was probably sung in the temple at Jerusalem, composed in the time before the exile. Its theme and outlook concerning creation is similar to the wisdom literature referred to in Proverbs and in Job.[10] The view it casts is, perhaps, the most appropriate place to begin in exploring this biblical theme.

Psalm 104 presents a grand view of God's creation, in all its majesty. It looks to the air (vv. 2–4) and then to the land, which has been separated from the waters (v. 9). The rich life of the earth and its creatures is ensured by the provision of water and the plants that grow (vv. 10–16). The sun and the moon bring night and day, and "measure the year" (v. 19). And there is a brief reference to the sea and its creatures (v. 26).

The dependence of all creation on its Creator is the climax of the Psalm:

> All of them look expectantly to thee
> to give them their food at the proper time;
> what thou givest they gather up;
> when thou openest thy hand, they eat their fill.
> Then thou hidest thy face, and they are restless and troubled;
> when thou takest away their breath, they fail
> (and they return to the dust from which they came);
> but when thou breathest into them, they recover;
> thou givest new life to the earth.
>
> Psalm 104:27–30

The striking feature about this creation Psalm is the humble role of humanity in the picture. In no way is the creation at the disposal of humanity; it is not created for humanity. And humanity's role within the creation is akin to that of other creatures. God, for example, makes springs and rivers so that animals might drink and so "the birds of the air nest on their banks and sing among the leaves" (v. 12). Likewise, the Cedars of Lebanon provide a home for storks and birds (vv. 16–17). The high hills are the haunt of the mountain goat (v. 18), while the boulders make a refuge for the rock-badger.

The grass grows for the cattle (v. 14), and green things grow also for humanity, to "bring bread out of the earth and wine to gladden men's hearts and oil to make their faces shine" (vv. 14–15). When the sun sets, the beasts of the forest and lions come out to get their food from God (vv. 20–21), and go back to their lairs when the sun rises. Then "man comes out to his work and to his labours until evening" (v. 23). In the sea, there are creatures beyond number, and "here ships sail to and fro" (v. 26).

The life and activity of humanity in creation appears almost incidental. Humanity's presence in, and dependence upon, the rest of creation mirrors that of other creatures. The only exception is the abrupt recognition that humanity is capable of spoiling this beautiful and harmonious creation; thus, "Away with sinners from the earth, and may the wicked be no more!" (v. 35). But the conclusion of this Psalm focuses on the glory of the Lord, and says, "may he rejoice in his works" (v. 31).

This biblical look into the creation, then, emphasizes not the initial acts of God that simply produce the creation, but rather the continual, preserving, and creative activity of God within the creation, and the dependence upon God for life that extends to all of creation, including humanity. God's primary purpose in creation, as seen in this Psalm, is not to provide a living environment for the sake of humanity; rather, the chief purpose of the creation's life is to glorify God.

Moving from Psalm 104, we turn our attention to the opening

chapters of Genesis. Most biblical scholars today agree that two streams of writing, originating at different times in the history of Israel, feed together into these chapters. Being aware of the historical roots and settings that produced these (as well as other) portions of scripture can deepen our grasp of their meaning and truth.

Genesis 1 through 2:4 completes the first account of creation. This passage, probably written during the Babylonian exile of Israel, is referred to by scholars as part of the Priestly source. For our purposes, we need to simply recognize that account as addressed initially to a people who had experienced exile—a people removed from the structures of religious, social, and political security and now surrounded by the claims of foreign gods and religions. Their faith was being severely tested; they were searching for their roots.

To such a people—then and today—Genesis 1 proclaims God as the Creator and Ruler of the world. And it announces that this God can be trusted. That trust begins with an understanding of the world as God's good and well-ordered creation.

This initial creation account in Genesis bears many striking similarities to Psalm 104.[11] Both accounts progress through creation, beginning with light, then the heavens or the firmament, and then the earth, which in Genesis is on day three (verses 5–18 in Psalm 104). Next in both comes day and night, and then the sea. In the Genesis account, the creation of all the land animals and humanity, which together share grains and fruit falls on the sixth day; Psalm 104 depicts the same close relationship but includes humanity earlier in verses 14–15. Both accounts conclude with declarations of praise and consecration to God.

Thus, Genesis 1 unfolds the gift of God's good creation. On six occasions before humanity is mentioned in verse 26, God surveys the creation and sees that it is good. All that is in the creation has a positive value for God simply for itself and not in reference to humanity. The life of creation, as in Psalm 104, is not given over to the caprices of humanity; nor is it for humanity to create. Rather, this creation gives life to all living things, including humanity. And that gift is from God, the Creator. Through the first twenty-five verses of the chapter we are given this picture of the inherently good gift of God's creation.

On the sixth day, beginning in verse twenty-four, humanity shares with the land animals the same day of creation. But here, unlike Psalm 104, humanity is placed in a relationship of "dominion" over the animals. Furthermore, humanity is described as being in God's image. These crucial verses, which give humanity a place of special significance in all the creation, deserve our careful attention.

First, what does it mean to be created in the image of God? Through the ages, endless theological speculation has centered around this phrase. But in the process, the initial meaning originally intended by the biblical writer, and understood by the hearers, has been overlooked. Theology concerning the image of God, while often illuminating, has drifted far from the biblical context of this verse.

It was a common experience of that time for a king to reign over a wide region. Obviously, he could not be physically present in the whole territory. But to solidify his reign in more distant regions, he would erect an image of himself. To the people, this meant that he ruled and reigned over that area, and that his purposes would be carried out. Old Testament scholar Gerhard von Rad describes this as follows:

Just as powerful earthly kings, to indicate their claim to dominion, erect an image of themselves in the provinces of their empire where they do not personally appear, so man is placed upon the earth in God's image as God's sovereign emblem. He is really only God's representative, summoned to maintain and enforce God's claim to dominion over the earth.[12]

This is the experience the Old Testament writers had in mind when they declared that humanity was created in God's image. Humanity is given a special and unique role in the creation. That uniqueness consists in humanity's calling to uphold God's intended purposes for the creation; humanity is to carry forth the claim that creation belongs to God. Announcing that humanity has dominion over the animals is not a pronouncement that gives humanity the right to treat animals in any way that is useful or desirable to them. On the contrary, dominion in Genesis means that humanity is given the Godly responsibility of upholding and protecting the life of the animal world, and to do so on God's behalf. As one biblical scholar, Odil Steck, explains in *World and Environment,* this biblical passage

certainly does not give man the right of autonomous and autocratic disposal over the animal world for his own self-chosen purposes, detached from God. . . . Man rules in this office as God's image, i.e., as God's steward in the world, which God created for permanence. Any exercise of rule on the part of man prompted by independent purposes, arrived at apart from God or in deliberate separation from him, and leading to the damage or even destruction of the foundations of the animal world, would be totally contrary to the intentions of what (this passage) has to say.[13]

This does not mean that animals are to be of no usefulness to humanity. Part of the structure of the creation includes an interdependence between all aspects of the creation, including humanity's dependence upon certain domestic, as opposed to wild, animals. Such animals are to be used for the tilling of the fields; animals also provide clothing for humanity. But it is a part of the limits, and the positive, preserving function of dominion in this passage, that animals are not even to be killed for food.[14] Verses 29 and 30 make clear that for both humanity and animals, plants, fruits, and grains are given for food.

This preserving responsibility toward creation, and specifically in this case toward animal life in creation, is culminated in the instructions to Noah to take two of every kind of animal into the ark. (It is only after the flood, resulting from violence in all the creation, that new decrees of God allow the taking of animal life for food, while strongly reinforcing God's care for the preservation of all creation. We shall explore this more fully in the next chapter.)

Thus humanity has a special role in God's creation—a role made clear in Genesis 1:26–28. But while popular interpretation begins with modern assumptions about nature being an object for humanity's exploitation and reads into this passage a justification of that position, quite the opposite is intended. The emphasis is on humanity's calling to uphold God's rule over the creation. The unique function of humanity, as contrasted to other creatures, is that humanity, in God's image, has both this power and possibility. But that is conferred upon humanity for the purpose of acting on God's behalf as a guarantor of the preservation and order of life for the whole creation.

In this passage, humanity's call to act as God's "steward" has its root. But contemporary calls for stewardship of resources are so vague, and seem capable of meaning so many different things, that one wonders how useful the term is. The fact that James Watt claimed he was simply being a wise steward in carrying out his policies toward the environment causes us to question whether the contemporary meaning of stewardship is at all close to the biblical understanding found in this passage.

The word stewardship is used today, both by Christians and non-Christians, to mean little more than good management. The assumption is that the world and its resources are at our disposal, to use as we best see fit. Our detachment from the world of nature and our manipulation of it is not questioned; our definition of stewardship tends to degenerate into merely carrying out this exploitation wisely, rather than foolishly. This thinking may offer some grounds for improving certain policies and practices affecting the environment, but it falls far short of the biblical meaning.

An analogy to the practice of slavery might be helpful here. There were certainly wise, sensitive, and even compassionate slaveholders in the South, as well as cruel and ruthless ones. But the Christian reaction to the question of slavery was not confined simply to urging slaveholders to be kind. Rather, it confronted the injustice of the basic relationship between slave and owner and called for a radical change. A new recognition of rights and a new pattern of relationship was the intended result.

Similarly, the Bible calls into question the prevailing pattern of humanity's relationship with the creation. Rather than nature serving as humanity's slave, humanity is placed into a whole new relationship with creation and called to safeguard its life for the sake of God. When stewardship means no more than simply being wiser slavemasters of nature—which often seems to be the case—the biblical meaning of the term is lost. Our call to be stewards of creation means biblically that basic ideas concerning our ownership of creation are abolished and replaced by the task of our bearing the image or likeness of God's rule over all the creation. As the Psalmist reminds us, "The earth is the Lord's, and the fullness thereof" (Psalm 24:1).

From this understanding of humanity's creation in God's image, we can grasp the clear meaning of the phrase "subdue the earth," in verse 28 of Genesis 1. Those three words have been removed from their scriptural context in order to justify the rape of the earth, or to blame the Christian faith for the results of this violation. But in actuality, the phrase merely extends the task of dominion in God's image. The "subduing" carried out by humanity is to have a positive function, upholding the order and intention of God's creation.

This becomes clearer when we recognize that the object of subduing is specifically the "earth," which means here not the world, but rather the ground. Loren Wilkinson, in the excellent study *Earthkeeping,* is correct in pointing out that the Hebrew word used, "kabash," has potentially a very strong meaning, such as tread down or conquer.[15] But this becomes more understandable when we reocognize that the focus is limited to the ground. And the purpose, reflected in verse 29, is to cultivate the ground for food: "I give you all plants which bear seed everywhere on earth, and every tree bearing fruit which yields seed; they shall be yours for food."

Certainly for a people at the dawn of creation, subject to the forces of nature and facing the task of establishing agriculture, instructions to take the ground under control in order to produce food would make sense. Further guidance might be needed for the style of agriculture—raping the earth as contrasted to preserving the earth's fruitfulness. And such guidance is given, as we shall see, as early as Genesis 2. But part of God's ordering of creation is that the earth brings forth food for humanity (and animals). Acting in God's image toward the earth includes cultivating the earth in order to bring forth this fruitfulness.

Two other observations seem noteworthy. First, remember that these words come before the portrayal in Genesis 2 of humanity's capacity for selfishness and sin. The positive intentions of creation, and humanity's role in it on God's behalf, are set forth in Genesis 1. Having dominion over the animals and subduing the earth, along with filling and increasing the creation with humanity's life, all are to carry forth the right and sustaining relationships of life in God's creation. At this point in the account, these right relationships are being established; the potential for their being broken has not yet surfaced.

Second, in Genesis 9, the Lord repeats the injunction given in Genesis 1:28 to Noah and his sons after the flood. But here, the phrase "subdue the earth" and "rule over" are conspicuously omitted. It may have been that at that point, in recognition of humanity's capacity for violence and selfishness, words which could be interpreted as condoning humanity's sinful misuse of the creation purposely avoided.

To summarize the view of creation affirmed in the account of Genesis 1–2:4, we can turn again to Odil Steck:

There can be no question of the world of animals being created for man's sake, let alone for the sake of his autonomous exploitation. If we want to find a formula, then [the Genesis writer's] intention is best represented by saying that the world is created by God for the sake of all life.[16]

Genesis now continues in its account of creation with the picture of God creating Adam and Eve and placing them in the Garden of Eden. This portion, beginning in Genesis 2:5 and continuing through the story of Cain and Abel, is thought to have been written during the time of David and Solomon, and is called by scholars part of the "Yahwehist" source. It is probably the oldest biblical picture of God's work of creation.

As in the other creation accounts, the world is bestowed by God as a gift. All life has its roots in the Lord. And here, in Genesis 2, that life is shown in a state of perfection. This picture of paradise is not meant to provoke nostalgia, but rather to remind us of the creation's need for God's blessing.

Humanity's intrinsic ties with the creation are made clear by God's creation of Adam out of the dust of the ground. The Hebrew word is "adamah," from which Adam's name is taken.[17] After Adam was created, the Lord "planted a garden in Eden" (2:8) and put him there. This verse, then, emphasizes the purpose of creation in providing a living environment to meet human needs, somewhat in contrast to the first two passages we have examined.

Adam's task in the garden, however, dispels the thought that creation is at humanity's disposal. Rather, Adam is to "till and keep" the creation. The Hebrew word for till, "abad," means serve, even to the point of "being a slave to."[18] "Keep," from the Hebrew "shamar," can also mean watch or preserve. Both terms strongly indicate a form of service on behalf of the creation. Rather than creation being owned by humanity, humanity is given the task of serving and preserving the creation. These words echo and amplify the meaning of being created in God's image from Genesis 1:26.

Serving and preserving the creation is rooted in the orientation of one's life to God. The view of Genesis is that the Lord blesses life, sets forth the values for life, and issues the promises for securing life—both for humanity and all creation. Life lived in relationship to the Lord God necessarily and naturally is a life that participates in sustaining the creation.

But in Genesis 2–3, we are made aware of another inclination of humanity—the desire to orient life around self-chosen purposes, apart from God. Life, then, becomes defined by humanity's search for power and ambition. For people living within the successful and prosperous kingdoms of David and Solomon, as well as for those living today in cultures that pronounce self-aggrandizement as their chief virtue, these words have a discerning relevance.

Genesis uses the expression "to be like God" (3:5) to describe this inclination. We can understand its meaning, in part, as the desire to claim God's prerogatives over life and creation. Humanity falsely believes that its life and the life of creation is at its own disposal, to do with as it selfishly desires. The first act of this rebellion involves the fruit of a tree in the garden. God's intentions for humanity's relationship to God and to creation are overturned. Adam and Eve decide they can live life and use creation as they please.

Rather than live in the image of God, serving as the representative of God's rule and purpose in the creation, humanity wants to be like God, making autonomous decisions about life and creation and then attempting to carry out those decisions by one's own power, for one's selfish purposes. Humanity attempts to rebel.

In this way, the Garden of Eden represents a potential coup d'etat by humanity against God. Just like ambitious colonels who plot to take over their leader's power for themselves, humanity makes a grab for God's own power.

This rebellion is played out in the relationship between humans and the rest of creation. Rather than preserving all life, humanity believes it can take life into its own hands; in the chapter that follows, Cain kills Abel. And rather than regard the life of creation as God's gift, humanity now tries to act as though it owns the creation.

What flows from this account of humanity's rebellious inclination is a picture of distorted relationships between humanity and the rest of creation. This is often called "the curse," and it is found in Genesis 3:15–19, which we will examine in the next chapter. The point made is that the desire to "be like God" results in a distortion of humanity's relationship with the rest of creation.

This account of the Garden of Eden and humanity's rebellion is traditionally referred to as the Fall. Often, we assume that from Genesis 3 on, humanity is locked into a pattern of sin and rebellion, which proceeds downhill until the coming of Christ. But that is not what this account meant through the history of the children of Israel in the Old Testament.[19] Rather, this passage sets forth humanity's decision to define its life apart from God, and the destructive results of that decision, which affect all God's creation. But Genesis 1 and 2 set forth the dependence of all life and humanity upon God's blessing, and the invitation to live life in the image of Yahweh, the Lord, and in the service of the creation. Together, these two themes set forth the framework for the relationship between God, humanity, and the creation. Humanity's temptation to claim power over life and creation for its own self-directed purposes is contrasted with the promise of the gift of a life lived in fellowship with the Creator for the sake of the good creation.

These themes continue through the Old Testament and into the revelation of Christ. But in Genesis, even the first three chapters cannot be taken in isolation, for specific themes concerning God, humanity, and the creation are developed and completed in the eight chapters that follow, as we shall shortly examine.

But first we should look at the question of *how* the creation came to be and, specifically, from what it was created. Our thinking about how and why God created the world carries implications for what God's relationship to the earth is now, and what it ultimately will be.

The commonly accepted explanation of how the creation came into being is *creatio ex nihilo*—the world and all that is was created by God out of nothing, as a free act of his will. Interestingly enough, no scripture can be cited to support this view.[20]

The history of this doctrine and its eventual wide acceptance by the church needs to be understood. The early church was confronted with the Greek, dualistic view of creation. Matter was eternally in existence, along with God. The process of creation came about by God attempting to form and mold this chaos of matter into the universe. In later Greek thought and its development in the West this dualism took on a moral tone. The good was the ideal, spiritual, ordering force of reality, while the disordered, rebellious forces of the material world were evil.

Christian faith did battle with such dualism, for it knew that such tendencies threatened the faith. First, God was not one divine eternal reality among others; God was the one, sovereign Lord over all. Second, evil was not an intrinsic, eternal part of the creation; it resulted, instead, from humanity's freedom. As St. Augustine said, to refute the Manichean dualists, "Evil is not a substance; it is the perversion of a nature that is essentially good."[21] All creation, fashioned by God, was fashioned as good.

To reject dualism, church thinkers determined that the world, rather than being created out of a pre-existent matter, was created out of nothing, or "ex nihilo." This thinking affirmed that God was the sovereign maker of everything that is, dismissed dualism, and rejected the idea that the material world was evil. In these ways, *creatio ex nihilo* preserved vital and essential Christian truths.

The doctrine has also been used to emphasize the distinction between the Creator and the creatures. Some thinkers held that the world emanated, or spontaneously flowed forth, from God. Christian thinkers wanted to guard against pantheism, which would equate the creation with God, so they used the doctrine of *creatio ex nihilo* to emphasize God's transcendence and essential difference from the creation. The creation was not the Creator; it came forth from nothing.

Historically, we can appreciate the function of this doctrine, but problems remain in applying it to views and attitudes that predominate in the modern world. For the main legacy of this teaching today, in my judgement, is to falsely underscore God's separation from the creation.

The doctrine suggests that, as if almost by a whim, God created the world and suspended it in the universe (which he also created out of nothing). Then God placed humanity in this scene.

If creation came from nothing, how can it have any intrinsic relationship to anything outside of itself? One can see how well this doctrine fits the scientific and mechanical view of the world, which reduces creation to nature, objectifies it, and seeks control over it. Starting with the idea that God first created the world out of nothing, it is easy to draw the analogy of God as a clockmaker, who sets the world ticking and lets it go.

Though *creatio ex nihilo* was intended to emphasize God's freedom and transcendence, its durability, in my judgment, is due in part to its compatibility with the world view developed by the Enlightenment and the rise of modern science. For very different reasons, they also sought to remove the notion of God's ongoing identification with the workings of nature.

This is ironic, because one of the original intentions of the doctrine was to emphasize the dependency of the creation on God—the sole source of all that is. But today, declaring that God made the world from nothing seems to fit well with modern notions of the world's autonomy: made from nothing, the world is connected to nothing outside of itself.

Even Karl Barth, who accepted the teaching of *creatio ex nihilo,* admitted that "within the sphere of the ideas possible to us *creatio ex nihilo* can appear only as an absurdity." George Hendry, in *A Theology of Nature,* replies to Barth, "This is surely an absurd statement; for it would have the effect of equating faith in God as creator with assent to an absurdity."[22]

Are there other interpretations of the roots of creation that safeguard Christianity from both dualism and pantheism, but that reflect more fully and biblically the relationship between God and the creation? I think so.

Of all the scriptures mentioned previously that have reference to the work of creation, none supports the doctrine of *creatio ex nihilo.* Many of those scriptures emphasize creation by and through God's Word. As developed in the Bible, this comes to mean far more than creation merely by command. Creating by Word means creating by expression. And God's Word, which brings forth the creation, finds ultimate self-expression in Christ. When the first chapter of John speaks of the Word present at creation, and states that "through him all things came to be" (John 1:3), this indicates that the Word carries forth God's creation. "All that came to be was alive with his life" (John 1:4). The creation through the Word is an expression of God. And the creation is linked to the incarnation.

As George Hendry writes, in commenting on this passage:

This was the beginning of a movement, which is in God himself, and in which he moves out from himself to the creation of the world, and in incarnation to restore it to himself. . . . The coming of the light in the Logos incarnate was a coming to his own, and by his coming the world, which was from God, was restored to God.[23]

We can understand the creation, then, as an expression of God. No analogy is perfect, but it may be helpful to consider the creation of works of art.[24] A painting, novel, or symphony is an expression of the artist. One would not say that the source of the painting is paint, or of the novel, ink, or of the symphony, musical notes. Rather, the source of work is the artist's conception. When you listen to Beethoven's Fifth Symphony, you are listening to Beethoven. That does not mean that the symphony *is* Beethoven; yet it is surely an expression of Beethoven, carrying in some way his life.

So may we understand the creation. All that is made by God is an expression of God's life. Its root and source is not "nothing," but rather God. This does not mean the creation is God, any more than the symphony is Beethoven. All pantheism is excluded. The distinction between Creator and creation is clear. Yet, we do not so sever God from creation as to suppose that the creation comes from nothing.

At this point our analogy breaks down. A work of art, once created, is finished; the process of creation is over, and the artist's activity is completed. But with God's creation, it is not so.

As we have seen, God continually upholds the creation, and God's acts of creation are ongoing. The creation depends continually for its life upon the Creator. Furthermore, the Creator's work with the creation is not yet completed. Its final form is yet to come.

This ongoing relationship between the Creator and the creation indicates a relationship far more interlocked than that of the artist and the work of art. But the point of the analogy is that creation is an expression of God; this expression had its source, and will find its final consummation, in God.

This way of viewing creation, of course, also destroys any sense of dualism and accomplishes one of the chief purposes, historically, of *creatio ex nihilo*. But seeing the process of God's creation as God's expression—rather than maintaining that creation was made out of nothing—seems to correlate with the suggestions of biblical writers and preserves their feeling of the intimate relationship between God and the creation.

In Romans 11:36 we read, "Source, Guide, and Goal of all that is—to him be glory for ever!" The source of all creation, rather than nothing, is God.

NOTES

1. Walter Brueggemann, *Interpretation: Genesis* (Atlanta: John Knox Press, 1982), pp. 16–17.
2. Paulos Gregorious, *The Human Presence* (Geneva: The World Council of Churches, 1978), pp. 26–27.
3. It is not my purpose here to enter the debate between those who believe in evolution as described by Darwin and those "creationists" who assert that the Bible offers a different, scientifically supportable, theory of origin. However, the most stimulating and valuable addition to this discussion in recent years comes from Jeremy Rifkin's *Algeny* (New York: Viking Press, 1983), and I would urge readers to consider his critique of Darwin and his explanation of cultural models for understanding nature.
4. For a general and insightful discussion of the plight afflicting theologies of creation, see George Hendry, "Eclipse of Creation," *Theology Today* 28, no. 4 (January 1972): pp. 406–425.
5. Brueggeman, *Genesis*, p. 26.
6. H. Wheeler Robinson, *Inspiration and Revelation in the Old Testament* (Oxford: Clarendon Press, 1946), pp. 12–16.
7. Ibid., p. 13.
8. For example, the *Catholic Biblical Encyclopedia* (New York: Joseph F. Wagner Press) states under "Creation" that "the primary purpose of creation is to manifest God's goodness to His creatures . . . and this goodness is to be glorified externally by them" (p. 245).
9. Robinson, *Old Testament*, p. 16.
10. Odil Hannes Steck, *World and Environment* (Nashville: Abingdon, 1980), p. 78.
11. I am indebted to Dr. Chris Kaiser at Western Theological Seminary for his unpublished study and observations on the similarities between these two passages.
12. Gerhard von Rad, *Genesis: A Commentary* (Philadelphia: Westminster Press, 1961) pp. 57–8.
13. Steck, *World and Environment*, p. 105.
14. Ibid., p. 106

15. Loren Wilkinson, ed., *Earthkeeping* (Grand Rapids, Mich.: Eerdmans), p. 209.
16. Steck, *World and Environment*, p. 106.
17. Phyllis Trible, *God and the Rhetoric of Sexuality* (Philadelphia: Fortress, 1978), provides a provocative and compelling interpretation of Genesis 1–2, pointing out that the Hebrew words for male and female ("ish" and "issah") are not used until after the formation of Eve in Genesis 2. Thus the "Adam" prior to that could simply mean a person from the earth, or "earth creature." In such an interpretation, the male in Genesis 2 would not have been created before female, but rather, male and female would have been created simultaneously, as is described in Genesis 1:26–28.
18. Wilkinson, *Earthkeeping*, p. 209.
19. See, for an example, Brueggemann, *Genesis*, pp. 41–45, for an explanation of how the Old Testament viewed this account.
20. George Hendry, *Theology of Nature* (Philadelphia: Westminster Press, 1980), p. 150, footnote 6: "It has been repeatedly pointed out that *creatio ex nihilo*, 'creation out of nothing,' is not found explicitly in canonical scripture. . . ." Scriptures sometimes thought to teach *creatio ex nihilo* directly, such as Genesis 1:1 or Hebrews 11:3, upon examination do not present such a view. The earliest direct reference is in 2 Maccabees 7:28.
21. Langdon Gilkey, *Maker of Heaven and Earth* (Garden City, N.J.: Doubleday, 1952), p. 51. Chapter 3 contains a good summary of how *creatio ex nihilo* developed historically as a doctrine, and the purposes it has served in church history.
22. Hendry, *Theology of Nature*, p. 147.
23. Ibid., p. 165.
24. Hendry discusses the act of creation as being analogous to creating works of art on pages 155–57. Scriptural references comparing creation to the art of pottery are found in Isaiah 45:9 and Jeremiah 18:1–10.

5. God's Covenant with Creation

In Eugene, Oregon, the host for a talk show over a Christian radio station was interviewing me on the subject of Christian steward-ship for the earth. Suddenly a call came over the air saying, "I don't see why you're spending all this time and energy talking about our care for the earth. Don't you realize that the Bible says the earth is cursed? You should just accept that. We can't do any-thing about it." The host then responded, "Yes, it's true, the Bible does say in Genesis 3 that the earth is cursed." Looking at me, he then declared, "We do have to keep that in mind, don't we? You wouldn't disagree, would you?"

I fumbled for a 30-second answer that would make sense. The words did not come easily. Both the caller and the host assumed, like millions of other Christians, that according to the Bible, God places the earth under a curse, begun after the fall and continuing until the end of time. That belief requires some careful biblical examination.

The "curse" found in Genesis 3:14–19 is divided into three parts. First, the serpent is consigned to crawl on its belly, and an enmity is created between serpents and people. It is doubtful that this means that snakes or "creeping things" are permanently as-signed any less value in God's view, since they were included in the ark, and other passages speak of all creation including creeping things praising the Lord (see Psalm 148:10). Rather, this points to the origin of alienation between humanity and part of the animal world.

The second portion of the "curse" concerns the pain of women in childbirth (3:16).

The most important part of these verses, for our purposes, is

Genesis 3:17–19, which deals with the earth or, more specifically, with the ground. In verse 17 we read, "accursed shall be the ground on your account." And later, "It will grow thorns and thistles for you, none but wild plants for you to eat" (3:18). Obtaining food will come only from sweat and hard work.

What these verses point to is a distortion in humanity's relationship to creation, and in particular to the ground, which results from humanity's rebellious inclinations. There is no suggestion that all the creation has lost its inherent goodness. The earth is not suddenly made evil. Such interpretations extend far beyond what is found in this text, and conflict with countless other scriptures testifying to creation's capacity and purpose to show forth God's glory.

Rather, this passage in Genesis, and others that follow, declare that humanity's disobedience produces the alienation of humanity from the creation. Harmony between humanity and the animal world shows the first signs of being broken. And most importantly, the ground does not bear the fruitfulness of the lush garden originally pictured. It is even suggested that this alienation will make agriculture futile; there will only be wild plants to eat.

The picture of broken relationships between God, humanity, and creation can be contrasted with the wholeness intended by God. The Hebrew word for this vision is "shalom." And that rich vision encompasses the unity of creation existing in right relationships as designed by the Creator. Walter Brueggemann offers a clear picture of what this means: "The central vision of world history in the Bible is that all of creation is one, every creature in community with every other, living in harmony and security toward the joy and well-being of every other creature."[1]

Shalom is the result of God's rule. It is what God established in the creation, and seeks continually to re-establish and renew. Apart from recognizing and responding to God as the source, guide, and goal of all life, humanity's relationship with creation becomes distorted and marked by unfruitfulness, alienation, violence, and chaos. This is the message of Genesis 2 through 4—a message first sounded in the midst of the proud kingdom of Israel, an Israel becoming confident in its own power and tempted to trust only in itself.

The writer of these Genesis chapters seeks to reveal what happens when this self-seeking will to power, a potential present in humanity, becomes unleashed. A pattern of destruction follows, breaking God's intended shalom, upsetting the relationships within the creation, turning people against one another, and estranging humanity from the rest of creation.

The picture unfolds even more graphically in the story of Cain and Abel. Cain is a "tiller of the soil" (4:2), but the Lord fails to receive his gift, while the gift of Abel, a shepherd, found favour (4:5). Cain murders Abel, and when confronted by the Lord he replies, "Am I my brother's keeper?" (4:9) The root word for keeper is the same as the Lord's instructions to Adam to "keep" the garden (2:15). But while Adam turned from the task of preserving creation, Cain now denies any calling to preserve even the life of his own brother.

The judgment on Cain underscores the connection between sin and humanity's relationship to the creation. "The Lord said, 'What have you done? Hark! your brother's blood that has been shed is crying out to me from the ground. Now you are accursed, and banished from the ground which has opened its mouth wide to receive your brother's blood which you have shed. When you till the ground, it will no longer yield you its wealth. You shall be a vagrant and a wanderer on earth'" (4:10–12). Violence between people destroys humanity's relationship to the earth.

Cain is exiled from the ground. With the soil no longer bearing fruit, he becomes a rootless wanderer, settling in "the land of Nod" (4:16), which means the land of wandering. In the next verse, we read that Cain begins "building a city," suggesting the alienation from the earth so characteristic of urban civilization.

From this point on in Genesis a downward spiral of violence and disintegration unfolds. Humanity's enmity within its ranks increases, as evidenced by Lamech's vengeful boasting (4:23–24). And from humanity's hostility, the whole creation is marred. A consistent theme emerges here, which is restated often in the Old

Testament. As summarized by author David Ehrenfeld, "If man does evilly, creation reacts."

By the time of Noah, "God saw that the whole world was corrupt and full of violence" (6:11). And in response, God "was grieved at heart" (6:6). The violence causing the creation to deteriorate was painful to God. (The word used for grieve, in fact, is the same word referring to a woman's pain in childbirth.[3]) God is tempted to blot out the creation. "The end of all flesh has come before me, for through them the earth is filled with violence. I am about to destroy them and the earth" (6:13).[4]

Yet, "Noah had won the Lord's favour" (6:8). When Noah is born, a prophetic word announces that through him the alienation present since Adam and Cain will be overcome. Genesis suggests that since the time of Cain, humanity has remained exiled from the ground, perhaps like Cain consigned to a wandering, rootless life.[5] But of Noah it is said, "This boy will bring us relief from our work, and from the hard labor that has come upon us because of the Lord's curse upon the ground" (5:29).

The Hebrew word translated here as "relief" appears elsewhere in the Old Testament as "comfort," especially with reference to the comfort that comes from the promise of the end of exile and God's redemptive work.[6] An example is the familiar passage prophesying the coming of the Lord in Isaiah 40, which begins, "Comfort, comfort my people."

This promise of comfort instead of exile, and reconciliation with the earth, is highlighted by the probability that this portion of the story of Noah, like Genesis 1, was written when the people of Israel were exiled in Babylon. Just as Israelites longed for a reconnection to the land that had been their home, so the promise seen in Noah points to the land being restored as the fruitful home for humanity, and all of God's creatures.

The account of Noah and the flood reveals the biblical theme of new creation, appearing here in the Old Testament's account of history's beginnings. The coming of the flood, caused when "the windows of the sky were opened" (7:12), suggests that the creation is returning to the state of watery chaos pictured at the beginning of Genesis 1.

As one Old Testament commentator writes,

> We see water everywhere, as though the world had reverted to its prime-
> val state at the dawn of Creation, when the waters of the deep submerged
> everything. Nothing remained of the teeming life that had burst forth
> upon the earth. Only a tiny point appears on the face of the terrible wa-
> ters: the ark that preserves between its planks the seeds of life for the
> future. But it is a mere atom and is almost lost in the endless expanse of
> water that was spread over the face of the whole earth. A melancholy
> scene that is liable to fill the reader with despair. What will happen to this
> atom of life?[7]

But the watery chaos does not overtake God's creation: the disobedience of humanity and the disintegration of the creation are
not the last words ending in a watery judgment. Instead, God's
resolve, God's commitment to his intentions regarding the creation, are shown to be steadfast. God "remembered Noah and all
the wild and tame animals that were with him in the ark" (8:1).
And God begins with them in a renewing re-creation.

God causes a wind to blow once again over the waters (8:2), as
in Genesis 1:2. The windows of the sky are closed, establishing the
earth again. And the dry lands appear, even as they were originally
separated from the waters in Genesis 1:9. The earth's vegetation
returns, as shown by the olive leaf carried back to Noah by the
dove.[8]

As Noah, his family, and the wider family of living creatures
come out of the ark, he builds an altar and makes a sacrifice to the
Lord. The Lord smells the soothing odor of the sacrifice and declares, "Never again will I curse the ground because of man"
(Genesis 8:21). "While the earth lasts, seedtime and harvest, cold
and heat, summer and winter, day and night, shall never cease" (v.
22). The curse is removed. The promise hoped for in Noah is
fulfilled.

God continues to recognize humanity's "evil inclinations," but
God restores humanity's relationship to the earth, promising its
fruitfulness and trustworthiness. In spite of the self-seeking evidenced within humanity, God chooses to remain faithful to the
creation. It is almost as if the waters of the flood purify and cleanse

the earth, offering to a humanity which had nearly destroyed the life of God's creation a fresh start, a new creation. And humanity's reconnection with the earth is shown by the simple statement at the end of the account: "Noah, a man of the soil, began the planting of vineyards" (9:20).

God re-establishes the creation and promises humanity that it can live and propagate into the future within this world. Life is secured, fashioned, and set forth by the Creator. Genesis 1:28 is repeated to Noah and his sons. "Be fruitful and increase, and fill the earth" (9.1 and 9:7). But as mentioned in the last chapter, the phrases "rule over" and "subdue the earth" are now absent.[9] Rather, a new concern emerges—constraining the potential for violence and self-destruction which had brought creation to the edge of doom.

Part of that violence had been expressed between animals and humanity, and a change is recognized in their relationship. Almost as if wild animals now perceive the predatory instincts within humanity, "fear and dread" fall on them, which was necessary then as today for their self-preservation (9:2). And animals become a source of food for humanity (9:3). Yet, rather than a sanction for unhindered exploitation of the animal world this is an elaboration of humanity's continuing calling to respect and uphold the ordering of God's creation.[10] The life-blood of all animals is the sacred gift of God (9:4), and humanity is called on again to live in God's image. Furthermore, because of that calling, every human life is of sacred value to God (9:6).

In this way, the calling to be in the image of God directs us not only to uphold positively the interdependent pattern of life in the creation, but also to resist directly the potential of violence within humanity, which can annihilate the creation. Now given a new beginning, creation continues to bear a sacred value, endowed by God.

This new beginning for creation is climaxed by the covenant the Lord establishes with it. Here is where God's covenant promises first begin. And God's covenant is established not just with people; rather, it is a covenant with all creation.

Five times in Genesis 9:7–18, this covenant is announced and redefined—a covenant between God and every living creature, with "all living things on earth of every kind."[11] Further, this covenant is dependent on God alone, not on humanity's response. It "stresses the unilateral initiative and sovereign grace of the covenant maker who 'gives' or 'establishes' the covenant,"[12] in contrast to other covenants that depend upon conditions which are imposed.

God sets forth this covenant with creation—it includes all that is given the gift of life; it underscores the trustworthiness of the created order; and it reconciles humanity to the earth. God is with the creation. God's purposes for the creation will endure. What God has made, God will not forsake. Rather, the creation will be renewed and redeemed. It will be won back to God.

That is what the rainbow means—the sign, God says, "of the covenant between myself and the earth" (9:13). And in spite of the clouds of potential violence and rebellion that persistently threaten the creation, the promise remains. This does not safeguard the world from ecological catastrophe now within view or from destruction by humanity's arsenals of nuclear overkill. Rather, it is the promise that ultimately this creation will fully be God's obedient creation. And it is an invitation for God's people to live in God's image, setting forth and upholding God's promises for the creation, against all the threats of violence. For "the bow shall be seen in the cloud" (9:14).

The story of Noah and the flood, then, serves to complete the picture of God and the creation that the first chapters of Genesis set forth, before the history of Abraham and the children of Israel. The crucial themes that emerge serve as a foundation for all that follows. The creation is linked to God's covenant. The shalom—that intended pattern of relationships between God, humanity, and the nonhuman creation—can be broken by humanity's self-seeking willfulness. Yet God moves to restore the shalom, inviting humanity back into its role of modeling and living faithfully according to God's rule over the creation.

The potential for humanity's rebellion is ever present. After

Noah plants the vineyard, he gets drunk on its wine. And humanity again attempts to "be like God" in the building of the tower of Babel. Yet God's faithfulness is steadfast; continually, God moves to "win back" or redeem the creation. God's covenant with Noah and every living thing signifies that the Lord's redemptive activity is riveted to all of God's work of creation.

This foundation reverses various theological assumptions—some of which have been held by evangelicals, others by traditional Protestant liberalism. First, the earth is not cursed. Adam's disobedience does not intrinsically change the character of God's good creation. Instead, the picture presented is that human rebellion will infect and mar the creation; yet God's grace acts to restore the proper fellowship between God, humanity, and all creation.

Second, God's work of creation is not simply setting the stage for the drama of God's relationship to humanity. Modern theology has stressed the mighty acts of God in history. The children of Israel were characterized by their faith in a God who works in history and who opens to the future new possibilities. These insights have made an important contribution. Yet when stressed, as has often happened, in a one-dimensional manner, they place the focus exclusively on God's relationship to humanity as the sole focus of God's redemptive work. In this framework, the first eleven chapters of Genesis, which are not regarded in any event as historical, become almost incidental. They serve as the backdrop, but the drama doesn't begin until the calling of Abraham, and God's covenant with him. Further, the significance of God's covenant promises become limited to a people, rather than extended to the creation.[13]

The scholar perhaps most responsible for stressing this dimension of the Old Testament, Gerhard von Rad, issued an important warning against making this an exclusive focus:

The greater part of what the Old Testament has to say about what we call nature has simply never been considered. If I am right, we are nowadays in serious danger of looking at the theological problem of the Old Testament far too much from the one-sided standpoint of an historically conditioned theology.[14]

The ark included the animals. God's redemptive activity in history is not detached from the concrete relationship of God's people to a land—to a soil, its vineyards, its produce, its animals, in short, to its fruitfulness or barrenness. Rather, God's redemptive work moves to transform, or set right, these very relationships between people and the creation as it calls for faith in God's steadfast love.

Third, God's relationship to what we call nature, or the nonhuman part of creation, is minimized if God's transcendence is overemphasized. It is frequently supposed that believing in Yahweh as the "God of history" meant that unlike competing deities, Yahweh was not intrinsically related to nature, and in this sense was transcendent. But such a view makes serious errors.

Ignored, for instance, are the deep and abiding declarations of creation's total dependence upon the Lord, and God's intimate involvement with creation, which occur, as we have seen, throughout the Old Testament. The Old Testament's understanding of God's transcendence was not one that severed God from the world of nature. Quite the opposite. Because all of the natural world depended upon the one God, various versions of polytheism, which identified various gods with different parts of nature, and dualism, the opposition of forces of evil and forces of good, were rejected. As Odil Steck writes, "The one God Yahweh is now, as creator, related to the whole of the natural world in general and to everything that lives in it."[15] God's transcendence, then, refuses to identify God with any specific forces in nature not because God is removed or detached from nature, but because the life of *all* creation depends directly upon the Creator.

Consider, for example, Elijah's confrontation with the prophets of Baal on Mount Carmel in 1 Kings 18. As the one altar is set up to the fertility god Baal, and the other to Yahweh, the contest is not between a god of nature versus the God of history. Rather, it is through "the fire of the Lord" that the whole offering of the bull, as well as the wood, the stones, the earth, and the water in the trench were consumed (1 Kings 18:38). The message was not simply that the god Baal was impotent, but that Yahweh, the God of the twelve tribes of Israel, was also the God who ruled over nature. The God who delivered the children of Israel from Pharaoh could be trusted as the God who could secure the life of a people settled in a new land.

Proclaiming faith in God as the God of history makes little sense unless that God is also the Lord of nature. This is why the Old Testament affirms that the God encountered in history is the Creator, and that the whole creation exists not for humanity, nor as a stage, but as the expression of God's glory, and thus as recipient of God's redemptive activity.

We may think of the relationship among God, humanity, and creation as a triangle:

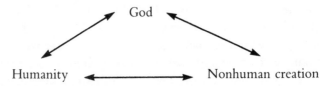

A break in one side of the triangle affects the other sides. God reaches out to both the human and nonhuman creation. But the willfulness of humanity, as distinguished from the nonhuman creation, has the potential for breaking all the links in the triangle. Rebellion against God causes a break in humanity's relationship to the rest of creation. And that rebellion even tries to pull the creation out of relationship to God and place it at the self-serving disposal of humanity. Similarly, a break initiated by humanity in our relationship to the creation ruptures our relationship to God. But God's redemptive activity is aimed at restoring the wholeness in each of these sides of the triangle.

The theme that humanity's rebellion against God wounds the creation occurs frequently in the Old Testament. For example, the prophets Isaiah (24:4–5) and Hosea (4:1–3) declare that humanity's disobedience causes the earth to dry up. Jeremiah repeats this connection when he writes, "but your wrongdoing has upset nature's order, and your sins have kept you from her kindly gifts" (Jeremiah 5:25).

Biblically speaking, then, violence toward others and rebellion against God alienate us from creation—and can even destroy the earth's fruitfulness and life-supporting capacity. We can reverse the equation. Our misuse of the creation breeds enmity between us and other people and alienates us from God.

This connection between rebellion and injury to creation is underlined by the manner in which Jewish law developed. For example, the law of *bal tashhit* ("do not destroy") is derived from Deuteronomy 20:19, which reads, "When you are at war, and lay siege to a city for a long time in order to take it, do not destroy its trees by taking the axe to them, for they provide you with food; you shall not cut them down." Commentary by rabbis on this part of the Torah expands the meaning of this instruction not only to the situation mentioned, but into a wide-ranging set of environmental regulations. As David Ehrenfeld has written, the prohibitions of the *bal tashhit* include

. . . the cutting off of water supplies to trees, the overgrazing of the countryside, the unjustified killing of animals or feeding them harmful foods, the hunting of animals for sport, species extinction and the destruction of cultivated plant varieties, pollution of air and water, overconsumption of anything, and the waste of mineral and other resources.[16]

Transgressors were likened to idolators, not allowed to participate in prayers, and virtually excluded from the community. The meaning of the *bal tashhit* to a religious Jew was summarized as follows by the nineteenth-century German rabbi Samuel Hirsch:

"Do not destroy anything!" is the first and most general call of God, which comes to you, man, when you realize yourself as master of the earth. . . . God's call proclaims to you . . . "If you destroy, if you ruin—at that moment you are not a man, you are an animal, and have no right to the things around you. I lent them to you for wise use only; never forget that I lent them to you. As soon as you use them unwisely, be it the greatest or the smallest, you commit treachery against My world, you commit murder and robbery against My property, you sin against Me!" This is what God calls unto you, and with this call does He represent the greatest and smallest against you and grants the smallest, as also the greatest a right against your presumptuousness.[17]

This summary of just one aspect of the law, as developed in the Jewish tradition, indicates the breadth of concern derived from the Old Testament for the preservation of the creation. Similar scriptures are those concerning the sabbatical year in Exodus 23:10–11, instructing the land to be left fallow every seventh year. In addition to respecting the soil and its own need for "rest," this practice also allows the land to provide for the needs of the poor and food for wild animals (Exodus 23:11). And the seventh day as a sabbath is observed "so that your ox and your ass may rest" (23:12).

The Year of Jubilee, described in Leviticus 25, extends the intention of the sabbatical year even further. Not only does the land rest; it is redistributed to prevent the hoarding and grasping of land, and to promote a just relationship between the land and people. Underlying these instructions is the fundamental understanding that the land, like all creation, belongs to God. "No land shall be sold outright, because the land is mine, and you are coming into it as aliens and settlers" (Leviticus 25:23). Because land is essential to life, and because it is God's gift, the land was to be preserved not just for Israelites, but for all who lived in it, including foreigners, orphans, widows, and the poor, as well as for domestic and wild animals.[18]

The stress on creation, and its specific expression in the land as God's gift, becomes a dominant theme through the Old Testament. Walter Brueggemann goes so far as to say, "The Bible itself is primarily concerned with the issue of being displaced and yearning for a place. Land is a central, if not the central theme of biblical faith."[19] The land is the domain of Yahweh, entrusted to the people only because of Yahweh's faithfulness to them, not because of their power or coercion.

But the warning of the prophets is that the land has a seductive power. The temptation is to cling to it, possess it, manage it, rule over it, own it—to treat it as though it were one's own domain, rather than to cherish it and only tentatively hold it as Yahweh's gift.

The kings typically wanted to accumulate, grasp, and control the land, which prompted prophetic warnings. An important illustration of this is the story of Ahab and Naboth in 1 Kings 21. Two conflicting views toward the land, and creation, are revealed. King Ahab proposed that he buy Naboth's vineyard. But to Naboth it was unthinkable to sell the land of his inheritance—meaning the land given, through his forefathers, by Yahweh. At Jezebel's prompting, Naboth is killed, and Ahab confiscates the vineyard. Elijah comes to Ahab pronouncing the word of the Lord: "Have you killed your man and taken his land as well?" (1 Kings 21:19). Then Elijah pronounces the Lord's judgment on Ahab.

Murder was only one result of the distorted relationship to creation. The principal sin was coveting the land, attempting to possess creation for one's own power and aggrandizement.

"Shame on those who lie in bed planning evil and wicked deeds and rise at daybreak to do them, knowing that they have the power," says the prophet Micah. "They covet land and take it by force"(Micah 2:1–2).

The gift of land to the people of Israel was conditional, dependent upon living within that land as if it were Yahweh's gift and they were Yahweh's people. But because they forgot this, choosing instead to grasp and possess the land as if it were their own, they lost it. That is the judgment announced by Jeremiah.

Israel's relationship to the land can portray, I believe, humanity's relationship to creation. Saving that creation, and our place within it, can come only by treating it as God's gift rather than our possession.

Furthermore, the Old Testament's continual declaration that all creation is God's gift lays the foundation for prophetic calls for justice. Establishing justice means restoring the right relationships within all creation.

Commonly, Christian ethics draws distinctions between concerns for justice between rich and poor and responsibilities for the care of the earth. And historically there has been tension between voices from the poor nations who demand that they be granted a more equitable share of the earth's bounty and voices from the rich nations expressing a concern for preserving and conserving the earth's resources. This tension, for example, was evident in the United Nations' first Conference on the Environment at Stockholm in 1972, and has been frequently present during international discussions of these issues.

Biblically, however, these issues are interwoven and inseparable. Old Testament pleas for justice are linked to restoring humanity's broken relationship to the creation. Injustice has its roots in seizing and controlling part of creation for one's own selfish desires, and thereby depriving others of creation's fruits, making them poor, dispossessed, and oppressed. The Bible judges these injustices to be sinful not so much because of the dignity of all persons (which the Bible, of course, affirms), but rather because of the conviction that the creation is God's possession. Because it is God's, rather than ours, no one is to be deprived of its fruits; neither is anyone to hoard its bounty. Unlike modern liberal humanism, the starting point of value here is not individual human rights, but rather God, and God's gift of creation. The poor and oppressed are to be given justice because the earth is the Lord's, and all who dwell therein.

All are to partake in God's shalom, so that the fruits of creation might confer the gift of life from God on all that God has created. Those who oppress the poor are not simply violating their rights —though in modern terms this is perfectly true; more importantly, such oppressors are violating and breaking the wholeness and peace of God's creation.

This perspective helps explain why many Old Testament passages about justice to the poor and oppressed appear side by side with hopes and promises of the earth's fruitfulness. This has nothing to do, of course, with modern capitalist ideas of simply increasing the size of the pie in order to meet the needs of the poor. Quite the opposite, these passages call for a new relationship between humanity and creation, and indicate that when justice and shalom within the creation are established, then the earth's fruitfulness and prosperity—meaning its ability to supply the needs of all—will break forth.

For example, Psalm 72, which is often read during Advent, begins,

> O God, endow the king with thy own justice,
> and give thy righteousness to a king's son,
> that he may judge the people rightly
> and deal out justice to the poor and suffering.
> May hills and mountains afford thy people
> peace and prosperity in righteousness.
> He shall give judgement for the suffering
> and help those of the people who are needy;
> he shall crush the oppressor. . . .
> He shall be like rain falling on early crops,
> like showers watering the earth.
> In his days righteousness shall flourish,
> prosperity abound until the moon is no more. . . .
> May there be abundance of corn in the land,
> growing in plenty to the tops of the hills;
> may crops flourish like Lebanon,
> and the sheaves be numberless as blades of grass.

Passages such as these help illustrate the breadth and depth of the meaning of shalom in the Old Testament. This vision unites the liberation of the oppressed with restoring and preserving the integrity of God's creation. Further, these two dimensions are essential to the Old Testament understanding of "peace," which is often the translation of the Hebrew word shalom. The threat to this shalom is the violent seizing of creation, the wanton taking of human and nonhuman life, and the suffering of those denied access to creation's gifts for nurturing life. This interlocking cycle infects the creation itself. As Hosea says, "You have ploughed wickedness into your soil" (Hosea 10:13).

The restoration of this shalom is not limited to justice between people. Again, the reference point is not just humanity, but the triangular relationship of God, humanity, and the rest of creation. A biblical ethic toward the environment is not based in humanity's relationship to the creation, but in God's. Thus, the concern for justice and the vision of shalom, while focused on re-establishing redemptive relationships between all people and the creation, reaches beyond to preserving and renewing the life of all creation as well. Habitat for the eagle and the grizzly, the richness of life in the Amazon rainforest, and the destiny of the snail darter all find protection in the vision of God's shalom, which liberates every oppressed part of creation, human and nonhuman alike.

At times in this chapter we have been speaking of creation and redemption in almost the same breath. Before concluding our survey of the Old Testament's insights concerning creation, we should examine the beautiful and sweeping passages in the second part of Isaiah, which link God's power as creator with God's work of redemption.[20]

Chapters 40 to 55 of Isaiah (sometimes called Second Isaiah or Deutero-Isaiah by biblical scholars) are thought to be written during the depth of the Babylonian exile to a people whose future seemed hopeless, whose present was bleak, and whose faith in the God of Israel was severely strained, almost shattered. In this setting, the prophet spoke majestic words of encouragement, consistently pointing to God's power as creator of heaven and earth, and the faithfulness of God to create a new future life—to bring about redemption. Central portions of these chapters set forth images of the Suffering Servant who will carry out this redemption.

God's trustworthiness as redeemer is underscored by remembering that "the Lord who is God, who created the skies and stretched them out, who fashioned the earth and all that grows in it, who gave breath to its people, the breath of life to all who walk upon it" (Isaiah 42:5). God will redeem his people; but that activity of redemption catches up the creation as well. "I will make a way even through the wilderness and paths in the barren desert, the wild beasts shall do me honour, the wolf and ostrich; for I will provide water in the wilderness and rivers in the barren desert, where my chosen people may drink. I have formed this people for myself" (43:19–21).

These themes echo throughout this portion of Isaiah. The focus is upon God's people being redeemed, and given new life. But God's actions of redemption are tied to God's work of creation. And thus, all creation responds to, and is included in, this redemptive activity. In 55:12–13 we read:

> You shall go out in joy and be led forth in peace.
> Before you mountains and hills shall break into cries of joy,
> and all the trees of the wild shall clap their hands,
> pine trees shall shoot up in place of camel-thorn,
> myrtles instead of briars;
> all this shall win the Lord a great name,
> imperishable, a song for all time.

Later in Isaiah, God's redemptive activity is described as the creation of "new heavens and a new earth" (Isaiah 65:17; 66:22). Violence shall be absent even in the animal world: "The wolf and the lamb shall feed together" (65:25). However we understand the fulfillment of passages such as these, we can clearly know that the redemptive activity of God brings forth the intentions of God's creation. The fellowship between God and humanity, humanity and creation, and all of creation with God springs forth and is restored by the God who creates and redeems.

NOTES

1. Walter Brueggemann, "Living Toward a Vision," in Edward A. Powers, *Signs of Shalom* (Philadelphia: United Church of Christ Press, 1973), p. 101.
2. David Ehrenfeld and Phillip J. Bentley, "Nature in the Jewish Tradition: The Source of Stewardship," unpublished manuscript, p. 6.
3. Walter Brueggemann, *Interpretation: Genesis* (Atlanta: John Knox Press, 1982), p. 77.
4. Bernhard W. Anderson, trans.
5. Adam is banished from the Garden of Eden, and the curse includes, as mentioned, that only wild plants will be food. Cain is then also unable to till the soil. From that point on in Genesis until after the flood, there is no mention of anyone engaging in agriculture, or in a fruitful relationship with the ground.
6. Brueggemann, "Living Toward a Vision," pp. 69–70.
7. Umberto Cassuto, *Commentary on Genesis,* vol. 2 (1964), p. 97, quoted in Bernhard W. Anderson, "The Relation Between the Human and Nonhuman Creation in the Biblical Primeval History," unpublished manuscript, p. 10.

8. Bernhard W. Anderson describes this comparison in a brilliantly moving manner in the manuscript cited above.

9. Some translations, such as the New English Bible, add the phrase "and rule over" in verse 7, but with a footnote. Such a translation is not accurate. The Hebrew is clear, indicating only the command to be fruitful and fill the earth, and not the words translated as "ruling over" and "subduing." Various commentaries offer conflicting explanations for this omission, but none seems convincing, in my judgment. The issue invites further attention by Old Testament scholars.

10. See for example Odil Hannes Steck, *World and Environment* (Nashville: Abingdon, 1980), p. 110.

11. Two different Hebrew words are used to indicate the scope of the covenant— "nefesh hayya," which the New English Bible translates variously as "every living creature," and "cul basar," which the New English Bible translates variously as "living things of every kind" and "all that lives on earth." Some translations use the term "all flesh." While this is a direct translation of the Hebrew words, "flesh" in this context and as used generally in the Old Testament, is not limited to human beings, but includes all living creatures. One could ask whether the scope of this covenant includes just animal life but not plant life, for example, but this would be too artificial a division, for the Old Testament understands that no animal life is possible without the living environment and habitat on which it is dependent. Thus, in verse 13 God says the covenant is established "between myself and the earth." I am indebted to Dr. Lester Kuyper of Western Theological Seminary for his assistance in examining the Hebrew terms in this passage and comparing various translations.

12. Bernhard W. Anderson, p. 6.

13. A concise and helpful statement of how theologies stressing the "mighty acts of God in history" have obscured the biblical concern for creation can be found in Walter Brueggemann, *The Land* (Philadelphia: Fortress Press, 1977), chapters 1 and 2.

14. Bruce C. Birch, "Nature, Humanity and Biblical Theology," Inaugural Address at Wesley Theological Seminary, 23 March 1977, p. 9. The rise of these concerns in von Rad's own thinking is certainly evident in his *Wisdom in Israel* (Nashville: Abingdon, 1972).

15. Steck, *World and Environment,* p. 124.

16. Ehrenfeld and Bentley, "Nature in Jewish Tradition," p. 15.

17. Ibid., pp. 18–19.

18. Steck, *World and Environment,* p. 120.

19. Brueggemann, *The Land,* pp. 2–3.

20. One thoughtful study of the themes of creation and redemption in Second Isaiah and throughout Scripture is John Reumann, *Creation and New Creation* (Minneapolis: Augsburg Publishing House, 1973). However, Reumann ends up concluding that creation is always understood through redemption, and argues for a narrowing of the implications of redemption to the creation of a new people, the church. His approach, in my judgement, primarily fights a losing battle in trying to so constrict the biblical perspective. Among his notable omissions are the story of Noah and the whole presence and impact of wisdom literature and its contribution to this theme—an omission he simply acknowledges in a footnote to the last chapter.

6. Redeeming the Earth

While working on this chapter in the library of Western Theological Seminary in Holland, Michigan, I noticed one day a new book that had just arrived titled *Jesus Christ—the Life of the World*. As I browsed curiously through its pages, my eyes fell upon a startling quotation: "The incarnation of Jesus Christ has to be seen in this cosmic sense, that God the Word has united himself not just to one human body, but to the spiritual-material cosmos as a whole."[1]

Is this what the New Testament teaches? In becoming a human person, does God reach out to restore a relationship to the world itself? When God the Creator acts as God the Redeemer, what is redeemed? Only believing people? What about the creation?

Raised and nurtured in a strong evangelical setting, I have been drawn to the New Testament as that place where the Bible truly becomes personal. Granted, the Old Testament contains inspiring stories of God's people; but in the New Testament, the focus on Jesus Christ as personal Savior made it, in my formative years, the heart of my study and meditation. The gospels (and especially John) presented the personal Christ, whom I had come to know as Savior. And the epistles were a rich resource of inward inspiration and guidance.

For years my most trusted and worn copy of the Bible was the New Testament, translated by J. B. Phillips. It was, in a real sense, all the Bible I really needed as an evangelical Christian. And the meaning of the New Testament was, in my view, focused almost exclusively on how individual Christians like myself, and the church as a body, were to understand personal salvation and live out their lives as believing Christians.

I treasure this personal heritage; through it I became bonded to faith in Jesus Christ as Lord of my life. Yet this tradition said very little about Jesus Christ, the life of the world. The "world," in fact, more often meant that which was to be overcome through Christ. And talk of redemption as having a cosmic scope was never heard.

This faith was intensely personal. And it should be. But it was never more than that. Thus the Bible was read and understood only as a guide to this inward, individual faith.

As with many other evangelicals, events in the world finally thrust me back into the Scripture searching for answers to questions which suddenly had begun to burn within me. The Vietnam War was chief among these events. But it was not only the war. As grievous as that slaughter was the enthusiastic complicity of the evangelical church.

So I, like thousands of others, began wondering if faith in Jesus Christ was only a personal matter. In asking that question, the Bible began to burst forth with new life for me. Its central concern for the poor, its cries for justice, and its message of peace—consistent themes all converging in the life, death, and resurrection of Jesus Christ—were discovered as central to biblical faith. Believing in Jesus as Lord retained its personal dimension, but could no longer be limited and bound there. Following this Lord led me as part of Christ's Body into the midst of the world's injustice, violence, and suffering.

That journey, begun years ago, still continues for me and for all those who have been addressed by this call of faith. "The politics of Jesus"—to quote the title of the hallmark study by John Howard Yoder[2]—have been firmly grasped concerning Christ's taking the part of the poor, his suffering love as opposed to violence, and his invitation to a new community organized around faithful allegiance to the Kingdom of God.

But now, for me, new dimensions are emerging beyond, or perhaps beneath, the politics of Jesus. For in this Lord, and in the New Testament witness to the meaning of his life, death, and resurrection, the fulfillment of all creation is revealed. The Lord over the lives of believers becomes far more; he becomes the life of the world.

The New Testament sets forth these truths in a variety of ways, which can deepen our faith and understanding. The themes we have discovered in the Old Testament concerning creation, humanity, and God are reflected and refined here. Let us consider several examples.

First, the teaching and ministry of Jesus call us to a new relationship with creation.

Those who are meek—humble and open, rather than defiant and grasping—will inherit the earth (Matthew 5:5). They do so through treating it as a gift rather than seizing it as one's possession.

We are not to worry about clothes and material belongings because we are to be free from the urge to secure God's creation as though it were our own. Creation is not ours to own, control, and mold according to our whims and desires; that maxim of every consumer society is overturned here, not by a call to renunciation and asceticism, but by a reunion with God the creator, and God's creation as gift. That is why we can learn from the lilies and the birds (6:26–28). They, after all, live recognizing that life is not their own, but an endowment by their creator. And the blessings of that endowment are far greater than anything we can gain by worrying over how we can be like God and gain power to use creation however we see fit.

Jesus also points to the gift of creation and the dependence of all life on the Creator as the basis for us to love our enemies. "Love your enemies and pray for your persecutors; only so can you be children of your heavenly Father, who makes his sun rise on good and bad alike, and sends the rain on the honest and the dishonest" (5:45, 46). "There must be no limit to your goodness, even as your heavenly Father's goodness knows no bounds" (5:48).

We hear echoes of the story of Noah, assuring seedtime and harvest, summer and winter, and setting forth a covenant with all creation. Accepting the creation as God's gift means realizing that God chooses to uphold even our enemies with life. Since they are not God's enemies, they must not be ours.

Deciding who can be hated whose lives can be taken was a consequence of humanity's attempt to be god over creation, seen in Cain's murder of Abel. Now, in these words, Jesus affirms that hatred and violence are irreconcilable with receiving God's gift of creation.

The parables and teachings of Jesus are full of illustrations drawn from the natural world. People often assume that this was merely an effective teaching technique within a society with agrarian roots. While that is true, more seems to be involved. The frequent appeals of Christ to the created world in his teaching underscores its trustworthiness, value, and integrity. Seeds grow when planted in fruitful soil. Houses should not be built upon sand, but on rock. A mustard seed, sprouting into fruitfulness and providing a home for birds, is like the Kingdom of God. A tree can be judged by the quality of its fruit. These references point to the fact that the creation possesses the qualities from which we can learn the deepest truths of life.

The intrinsic value of creation, simply because of its relationship to God, is indicated not only by the reference to God's care for the lilies and the birds in the Sermon on the Mount, but also by Jesus' statement that no sparrow falls to the ground without God's knowledge (Matthew 10:31). The content of Christ's teaching reveals an invitation to re-orient our relationship to his Father's creation.

Some of Christ's parables have obvious ecological applications that are often overlooked. For instance, the teaching of the parable of the talents in Matthew 25:14–30 is demonstrated by this true story. In 1881, an American missionary brought four pounds of peanuts to Shantung Province in China. He gave two pounds each of this new seed, previously unknown to the region, to two Chinese converts. The first convert ate his entire first-year crop. But the second convert saved the harvested seed, and even passed some on to other neighboring farmers. Eventually, Shantung Province became one of the leading peanut-producing regions of the world. The "talents" were shared and thus fruitfully multiplied by the second convert, rather than being selfishly hoarded.[3]

Each of the first three gospels contain Christ's parable about the person who planted a vineyard, and then leased it to tenants (Matthew 21:33–46, Mark 12:1–2, Luke 20:9–19). He then sent servants back to gather in the fruitfulness of the vineyard. But the tenants tried to seize control. They beat and killed the servant. Finally, the owner sent his only son, whom he thought they would certainly respect. But the tenant said, "This is the heir. Come on, let us kill him, and the inheritance will be ours."

The parable has a meaning and application on many levels. But the most obvious seems often neglected. For this is a story about God's creation and humanity's role. God expects the tenants, or stewards, to treat the vineyard he has planted as God's. He is the owner, we are his servants. That is the meaning of being created in God's image.

But instead, humanity wants to grasp control. We bring creation to the brink of nuclear destruction. We assume the role of mastery over the creation of life. We imperil the earth's ability to support life and the lives of millions through wanton selfishness.

Christ comes to reclaim the ownership of the creation, and of our lives. But he is rejected and killed. Yet, out of his death—from this ultimate self-giving—there comes life. Death is defeated, and creation is restored as his.

The ministry of Jesus, as well as his teaching, points to this restored relationship with the creation. Many of his miracles express not only simply a power over nature, but rather point to renewing a fruitful relationship with the gifts of creation. Thus, the hungry are fed when two fish and five loaves of bread are shared; water is turned into wine to celebrate a wedding; and fish fill the nets of the disciples when they respond to Jesus.

When Mark pictures Jesus as stilling the storm, with the wind and the sea obeying him, and feeding the crowd who had followed him into the Gallilean wilderness, the message is clear. Yahweh, whose Spirit blew over the waters at creation, who blew back the Red Sea, and who provided manna to the children of Israel in the desert, is uniquely present in the life of Jesus. The creator and sustainer has become flesh.[4]

The healing miracles of Jesus underscore this truth. The root word used most frequently in the New Testament to speak of healing means "to save" and is the source for the word "salvation." The healings of Jesus, so central to his ministry, point to a restoring of God's intended purposes in people's lives and in the world. These healing acts are signs that a new order, the Kingdom of God, is breaking into our midst. The aim of this Kingdom is to re-establish God's reign over all the creation.

Second, humanity's creation in the image of God is restored in Jesus Christ. Listening to Jesus' proclamations of the Kingdom of God being at hand reminds us of the intended meaning of "dominion" in Genesis 1:26–28. Christ calls us to a life obedient and receptive to God's rule over creation. So it is is not surprising that New Testament writers described Jesus as the "image of God." Second Corinthians 4:4 describes Christ as "the very image of God," and then refers to God's act of creation in Genesis 1. Colossians 1:15 repeats this description.[5]

In Hebrews 2:5–10 we find a revealing reference to Psalm 8. This Psalm is an echo of Genesis 1, speaking of humanity as being created "a little less than a god," and giving humanity dominion over creatures, "putting everything under his feet" (v.5). But the writer of Hebrews explains specifically how humanity has failed in this task. "But in fact we do not yet see all things in subjection to man" (Hebrews 2:8–9). The intended relationship between humanity and creation—a relationship characterized by the harmony of God's sovereignty—has been ruptured. But, Hebrews then declares, we do see Jesus, "who for a short while was made lower than the angels, crowned now with glory and honour because he suffered death" (2:9). Jesus Christ is the image of God, restoring through his life, death, and resurrection the reign of God.

The well-known passage in Philippians 2:5–11 also provides an echo of this theme. Christ is said to be in the "form" or "divine nature" of God. But this was expressed through Christ pouring himself out, in emptying and serving. Bearing the likeness of God means a posture of service, rather than a striving for power. Instead of grasping equality with God, Christ pours out his life. Just as God's life is poured out to the creation in a constant giving of life, so the Son of God's life is marked by service rather than self-centeredness.

In seeing the image of God restored in Jesus Christ, we discover that the definition of acting as God's representative is a posture of servanthood toward all the creation.

Third, God's redemptive work in Jesus Christ reaches out to the whole creation. Most Western theology has interpreted redemption as applying simply to people. This limited focus has its roots in the view of the Old Testament as primarily the story of God's covenant with a people, his liberation of a people, and God's mighty acts in history. Absent are other Old Testament themes stressing God's presence with creation, God's intentions for all creation, God's covenant with all living things, and the relationship of God's people with the creation. When these themes are neglected in the Old Testament, it becomes easier to miss them in the New Testament.

The words of one Old Testament scholar, Norbert Lohfink, are an important reminder of the understanding found there:

When the world is, in fact, what the Creator has always wanted it to be, then "salvation" comes into being . . . a concern for "salvation" that does not envisage responsible concern for completing God's work of creation is foreign to (this) theology.[6]

We have seen clearly how the Bible portrays the interdependent relationship between God, humanity, and the whole creation. Just as humanity's rebellion spreads like an infection into all creation, God's redemption in Christ extends to humanity and creation, restoring them in relationship to each other, and to God.

Thus in Colossians we read of Christ that "through him God chose to reconcile the universe to himself" (Colossians 1:20). The scope of Christ's redemption is cosmic.[7]

In Jesus Christ the power of sin and death is overcome. The creation is reconciled to God. Redemption reaches to claim all creation as God's own.

Humanity, the nonhuman creation, and even the fallen, evil powers in the cosmos, are won back to God. When the New Testament declares that Christ has triumphed over the principalities and powers, and put everything in subjection beneath his feet, it proclaims Christ's defeat of all those powers that try to exercise sovereignty over creation apart from God.

The power of sin seeks to destroy humanity's fellowship with God, breed enmity among human beings, alienate humanity from creation, and infect creation with disorder and violence. The power of God's redemption in Jesus Christ restores fellowship between creation, humanity, and God.

The frequent New Testament references to all things being made subject to Christ through his death and resurrection (such as Philippians 3:21, Ephesians 1:22, 1 Corinthians 15:25–28, Hebrews 2:8–9) also emphasize the scope of redemption as including the whole cosmos. To quote one biblical scholar:

Paul corrects a soteriology which is oriented solely toward the redemption of the individual. . . . This rule of God over the whole world is more than the new existence and hope of the individual. . . . Christ is now, already, not merely the one to whom the individual Christian and the church belong, but the one to whom the world belongs.[8]

Redemption's reach to all creation resounds in Romans 8:19–21. A helpful translation of this difficult, yet crucial passage is provided by Professor C. F. D. Moule:

For creation, with eager expectancy, is waiting for the revealing of the sons of God. For creation was subjected to frustration, not by its own choice but because of Adam's sin which pulled down nature with it, since God had created Adam to be in close connection with nature. But the disaster was not unattended by hope—the hope that nature, too, with man, will be released from its servitude to decay, into the glorious freedom which characterizes man when he is a true and obedient son of God.[9]

Our redemption through Christ means that we are restored in our relationship to the creation. The whole creation becomes new to us. As one author puts it,

Redemption addresses itself not only to man's sense of guilt, but it addresses itself to man's fractured relationship to the material world. . . .

Man is now set free from the possibility of simply utilizing Nature for his own ends. Nature is no longer his object, but his companion.[10]

Fourth, in Jesus Christ, God acts to save the world. In John 3:16–17, we read the famous passage that has served as the magna carta of evangelicalism. It was the first passage of Scripture I memorized as a child:

God loved the world so much that he gave his only Son, that everyone who has faith in him may not die but have eternal life. It was not to judge the world that God sent his Son into the world, but that through him the world might be saved.

To our Western and largely evangelical ears, we have heard and read this passage as if "world" meant "people." And when people are saved, they are saved from the world.

Our concept of salvation consists of God plucking people up and out of a world headed for destruction. The image is like a rescue helicopter sending down a line for passengers on a burning, sinking ship to grab onto and be hoisted to safety.

But this is not what Jesus says in the third chapter of John. Rather, he has been sent by God to save the whole world—the entire creation. Salvation means saving our ship.

Our difficulty stems from thinking that humanity exists apart from, and independent of, the rest of the world. By thinking of humanity as separate from the rest of creation, we then assume that we can be saved while creation is destroyed. Further, we think of salvation as a spiritual reality divorced from physical reality; our souls are saved though our bodies are destroyed.

But Christianity preaches the resurrection of the body and the salvation of the world.

The theology of the Eastern Orthodox church can greatly enrich us on these points. In general, Eastern thought—including most non-Christian Eastern religions—has never assumed the dichotomy between humanity and nature so prevalant in the consciousness of the West. Rather, in the words of Joseph Kitagawa, "Unlike Western man, who believed himself to be situated somewhere between God and the world of nature, Eastern man has always accepted the humble role of being a part of nature. . . . Man has value, but in himself he has no separate destiny apart from nature."[11]

Christianity, we must recall, is also, in its origins, an Eastern religion. Our brothers and sisters from the Eastern Orthodox tradition bring to their theology a far richer—and I suspect more biblical—understanding of how God's redemption extends to the creation. They have always asserted that in the incarnation, God in Christ acts to restore the world, and call it back to himself. Redemption is the promise of creation being made whole and new, as well as our own lives. As contemporary Orthodox theologian Paulos Gregorios writes, "Human redemption is inseparable from the redemption of time and space as well as of 'things.' "[12]

Key to understanding the New Testament's teaching concerning salvation and the world is realizing the various meanings the term "world" has in Scripture. The New Testament term most often translated as "world" is the Greek word "cosmos." This word appears seventy-eight times in the gospel of John alone, twenty-two times in 1 John, forty-six times in Paul's letters, and fifteen times in the first three gospels.[13] But its meaning is not always the same. In fact, there are three different meanings for the word in the New Testament.

First, "world" means the whole universe, or heaven and earth, or the totality of all that is created. For instance, When John writes in the first chapter that the Word "was in the world" and that this world "owed its being to him" (John 1:10), the meaning is all creation. Likewise, Christ's declaration in John that he is "the light of the world" (8:12, 9:5, 3:19, 12:46, 1:9) carries this same meaning. The same is true of passages speaking of Christ being sent into the world, or sent into the whole creation (10:36, 11:27, 12:-46, 16:28, 18:37, also 1 John 4:9).

A similar meaning is found in the epistles, although the Greek world "cosmos" is not used when we read, for instance, "the *whole universe* has been created through him and for him" (Colossians 1:16), or "He has put *all things* ("panta" in Greek) in subjection under his feet" (1 Corinthians 15:27). The passage in Hebrews

2 examined earlier has the same meaning: "all things" is the whole creation.

John's words, then, that God's love for the whole world prompts the sending of his Son, and that world is to be saved, points to and includes the whole creation.

A second meaning, more limited in scope, is also present in the New Testament. "World" at times signifies simply the place where humanity lives or the earth that is inhabited and can be controlled. For instance, when Jesus asks, "What does a man gain by winning the whole world at the cost of his true self?" (Matthew 16:26, Mark 8:36, Luke 9:25), he certainly means something less than the entire created universe. In a similar vein, "world" may refer just to all the people who live in the world. Sometimes, then, "world" can be simply equated with people. However, the New Testament generally does not limit the meaning of world so narrowly.

The third meaning of "world" in the New Testament is probably the most responsible for obscuring our understanding; yet in some ways it is the most crucial of the three. "World" also means the whole sphere of life lived apart from God. This can refer to creation as it is infected by humanity's rebellion; it also signifies the structure and organization of humanity's life in opposition to God. Thus, Paul writes about "the whole world" being "exposed to the judgement of God" (Romans 3:19). And in a passage famous for radical discipleship, Paul urges Christians to "be not conformed to this world" (Romans 12:2). The New English Bible perhaps catches its meaning better, saying, "Adapt yourselves no longer to the pattern of this present world." In other words, don't organize your life according to the structures and values in society that are formed apart from God. (Actually, the Greek word in this case refers to this "age" rather than the "cosmos.")

This same meaning is reflected when James warns, "Have you never learned that love of the world is enmity to God?" (James 4:4). In this sense, Christ says his followers are "strangers in the world, as I am" (John 17:16). So Christians are counselled, "Do not set your hearts on the godless world" (1 John 2:15). It is this "godless world"—life lived apart from God—which has rejected Christ. Nevertheless, Christians are still called to live in the midst of this godless world, yet not to be part of it, "because you do not belong to the world" (John 15:19).

Yet the world lived and organized apart from God has been conquered by Jesus Christ (John 16:33). And this world, this realm of life without God, is to see through the life of believers that God sent Christ for the salvation of the world (John 17:21,23). Thus, the world, in this sense, means the place of God's saving activity and grace. It is a world apart from God but won back to God through Christ.

Humanity's attempt to "be like God," organizing and living life as if God is not, results in a reign of sin that threatens all creation with destruction. But God's salvation in Jesus Christ breaks the reign of that sin; the power of the world of life apart from God is overcome. Creation again becomes a gift. Salvation comes to the world.

Fifth and finally, the New Testament declares that Jesus Christ is the life of the world. The universe is centered in Christ; its unity and cohesion exists in him. The coming of Christ into the world reveals that the life of all creation is centered in the new creation inaugurated by the Son of God.

One of the earliest creedal hymns of the church is echoed, in all likelihood, in 1 Corinthians 8:6, where Paul writes: "Yet for us there is one God, the Father, from whom all being comes, towards whom we move; and there is one Lord, Jesus Christ, through whom all things came to be, and we through him." Christ is the mediator not just of our lives, but of the whole creation. Through him, the creation is sustained in its life and its fellowship with the creator. Hebrews portrays Christ the Son as the one whom God "has made heir to the whole universe, and through whom he created all orders of existence: the Son who is the effulgence of God's splendor and the stamp of God's very being, who sustains the universe by his word of power" (Hebrews 1:2–3). These same truths resound powerfully, as we saw earlier, in the first chapter of John's gospel.

Such New Testament passages take up the insights of the Old Testament's wisdom literature regarding God and creation. In fact, we can say that the two contrasting Old Testament themes of redemptive salvation history and wisdom's emphasis on God's presence in the creation are brought into a unity in Jesus Christ.[14]

In the incarnation of Jesus Christ, God's life takes on flesh and blood. The Spirit is united with matter. The whole of creation is opened to transformation because it has been impregnated with the very life of God. "My flesh is true food, my blood is true drink" (John 6:55). As Alexander Schmemann writes:

It is only when in the darkness of *this world* we discern that Christ has *already* "filled all things with Himself" that these *things,* whatever they may be, are revealed and given to us full of meaning and beauty. A Christian is the one who, wherever he looks, finds Christ and rejoices in him. And this joy *transforms* all his human plans and programs, decisions and actions, making all his mission the sacrament of the world's return to Him who is the life of the world.[15]

NOTES

1. Ion Bria, ed., *Jesus Christ—the Life of the World* (Geneva: The World Council of Churches, 1982), p. 60.
2. John Howard Yoder, *The Politics of Jesus* (Grand Rapids, Mich.: Eerdmans Publishing Company, 1972).
3. Ghillean Prance, "Missionaries as Earthkeepers," *Radix* 14, no. 3 (November–December 1982): p. 22–25.
4. See the description of these and other events in Mark in Norman Young, *Creator, Creation, and Faith* (Philadelphia: The Westminster Press, 1976), pp. 73–4.
5. See the brief discussion of Christ as the "image of God" in Walter Brueggmann, *Interpretation: Genesis* (Atlanta: John Knox Press, 1982), p. 34. Odil Hannes Steck, *World and Environment* (Nashville: Abingdon, 1980), differs from Brueggemann regarding Colossians 1:15, stating that this is not derived from Genesis 1:26–8. See pp. 253–254.
6. Norbert Lohfink, "Creation and Salvation in Priestly Theology," *Theology Digest* 30, no. 7 (Spring 1982): 3–6.
7. Literature regarding the "cosmic Christ" is extensive. The cosmic dimensions of redemption were underscored in an important way by Joseph Sittler's address to the New Dehli Assembly of the World Council of Churches in 1961, found in "Called to Unity," *The Ecumenical Review* 14 1961–62): 177–187. Sittler further explored these themes in his important work *Essays on Nature and Grace* (Philadelphia: Fortress Press, 1972). An extensive bibliography on the subject is found in John Reumann, *Creation and New Creation* (Minneapolis:

Augsburg Publishing House, 1973), though Reumann's purpose is to argue for a narrower understanding of these themes. He does not succeed, in my judgment, in diminishing the sweeping scope of several New Testament passages dealing with redemption.

8. See W. Schrage, "Die Stellung zur Welt bei Paulus, Epiktet und in Apokalyptik. Ein Beitrag zu I Kor. 7:29–31," *Zeitschrift für Theologie and Kirche* 61 (1964): 127–128, quoted in Steck, *World and Environment,* p. 248.

9. C. F. D. Moule, *Man and Nature in the New Testament* (Philadelphia: Fortress Press, 1967), pp. 9–10.

10. James C. Logan, "The Secularization of Nature," in *Christians and the Good Earth* (Alexandria, Va.: The Faith-Man-Nature Group), p. 123.

11. George S. Hendry, *Theology of Nature* (Philadelphia: Westminster Press, 1980), p. 198.

12. Paulos Gregorios, *The Human Presence* (Geneva: The World Council of Churches), p. 81.

13. *Theological Dictionary of the New Testament,* G. Kittel, ed. (Grand Rapids, Mich. Eerdmans, 1965), article on "cosmos," vol. 3, pp. 867–895. This has been the source of helpful insights regarding the New Testament's use of the word "world."

14. Much more can and should be said about the contribution of wisdom literature in the Old Testament and its influence in various New Testament passages, including many we have explored. I am indebted to the work of Dr. Robert Coughenour, Academic Dean of Western Theological Seminary, for his work in this area and his manuscript, presently in process, on the themes of wisdom literature in the Old Testament and their effect on the New Testament.

15. Alexander Schmemann, *For the life of the World* (St. Vladimir's Seminary Press, 1973), p. 113.

7. The World's Future

When does the world experience God's salvation? Does this happen only at the end of time? Do we know this only in hope at present? Between now and the end of the age, what is changed because of Christ's redemption?

The church today is in the midst of an intense struggle to understand its role in the future of the world. Such a challenge of course, is as old as the people of God. But new historical circumstances shape the nature of the church's current attempts to fashion a theology of the future.

On the one hand, liberation theology and "theologies of hope" have thrust the issue of history's future movement before the church with a new urgency and passion. The God who delivers and liberates opens the future to new possibilities. In the midst of the struggle by the poor and oppressed for justice, the signs of this new future can be found. And it comes within history—not at its end. Biblical passages about judgment announce God's condemnation of unjust and oppressive forces in the world, which are to be overthrown as history moves toward God's kingdom. Versions of these themes have emerged among many Christians committed to the biblical call for social justice.

At the other extreme, millions of Christians expect injustice, violence, ecological deterioration, and the probability of nuclear war to get worse, and believe this is what the Bible teaches. In fact, headlines proclaiming imminent disasters are welcomed as signs that the world is closer to its end, and to the second coming of Christ. The dawning of God's kingdom, according to this view, lies nowhere within this history, but will come only after Christ's return initiates a new beginning. The popularity of these views, particularly among many evangelical Christians, is demonstrated by the sale of millions of copies of books such as Hal Lind-

sey's *The Late Great Planet Earth* and by the loyal audiences drawn
to television evangelists such as Pat Robertson, Jerry Falwell, and
many others who proclaim a theology of "end times."

Traditionally, a majority of evangelicals in this century have
held such a view concerning the return of Christ, which is called
premillennialism. In general, Christianity teaches that human history as we know it will culminate and end with the return, or
second coming, of Christ and the final judgment. Premillennialists, however, believe that upon Christ's return, he will inaugurate
a rule of peace and righteousness on earth for a thousand years—
the millennium. After that, the final judgment will be executed,
with eternal life or death for all. Revelation 20:1–6 is the key biblical passage on which this belief rests.

Until this time, all the world will continue on an escalating
downward spiral, gaining momentum as evil reaches a cosmic crescendo. Wars, earthquakes, natural disasters, and famine are all
signs confirming, ironically, that history is moving according to
God's plan, and bringing the world closer to Christ's return.

Many premillennialists also hold to what is called a dispensational interpretation of the Bible.[1] This view, originated by John
N. Darby in the nineteenth century, places a heavy emphasis on
interpreting various Scriptures as prophetic, or predictive, of
events to transpire in the future. Thus, Old Testament prophets
such as Isaiah, Hosea, Amos, Ezekiel, and Daniel hold the hidden
keys to understanding the events unfolding in the twentieth century. In addition, dispensationalism regards different passages of
Scripture as applying only to certain times in history. For instance,
consider a passage like Isaiah 11, which reads, "Then the wolf shall
live with the sheep, and the leopard lie down with the kid; the calf
and the young lion shall grow up together" (Isaiah 11:6). This is
simply a description of the millennium, and has relevance only to
that time. Furthermore, critical passages such as Christ's teachings
about the Kingdom of God, and the style of life and love it requires, are also understood by dispensationalists as applying to the
time when Christ returns to establish his thousand-year reign on
earth.

The millennium will consist of an actual rule of Christ on earth, over all the nations and peoples of the world. During that time, creation will be restored to fruitfulness and harmony, and peace shall reign. The biblical promises for creation's redemption find their fulfillment on earth, but only during the millennium, after Christ's return.

We can graphically picture the premillennial view as follows:

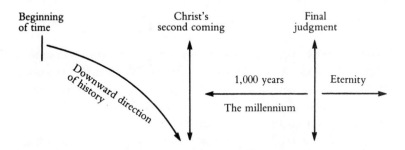

The church has lived through many ages when its own persecution, combined with the ungodliness of the times, have made a premillennial view seem persuasive and compelling. But other historical experiences of the church have given rise to alternative views.

When the Emperor Constantine came to power in the fourth century and converted to Christianity, the church's view of the future shifted decisively. Suddenly, future promises of a reigning Kingdom brought by God seemed to be present. In this context, postmillennialism developed, and was the dominant view of the church into the Middle Ages.

Postmillennialism asserts that the thousand-year reign of Christ begins on earth before the end of history. God's purposes are progressively accomplished as this reign is extended, perfecting the world and bringing it closer to its final fulfillment. While premillennialism tends to postpone all the effects of God's redemption of the creation until after Christ's second coming, postmillennialism looks for nearly all the effects of this new kingdom within the present age.

A picture of the postmillennial view appears on the next page. Unlike the era in which Christendom reigned, in our time the

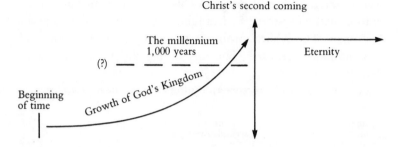

naiveté of postmillennialism seems obvious. History is not moving progressively toward a utopia. What the world calls progress seems to move civilization further away from the Kingdom of God, rather than closer to it. And the danger of the postmillennial view has been to identify forms of Christendom—ranging from Constantine's Empire to the New World in North America—with the Kingdom of God, baptizing its order, power, and even its armed might with divine blessing.

But are we then thrown into the arms of an apocalyptic premillennialism? Are we to agree that the Bible's vision for the world's future is marked solely by catastrophe and disaster? I think not.

The most extreme form of this perspective, dispensational premillennialism, gained a hold among fundamentalism primarily through the conversion of evangelist Dwight L. Moody to this view. Later, dispensational premillennialism was incorporated into the millions of Scofield Reference Bibles, whose interpretations were seen as infallible as the Scripture itself early this century.

Today, many leading evangelical scholars and leaders discredit this position. Equating contemporary events in the Middle East to obscure references in Ezekiel seems bizarre to growing numbers of conservative Christians. Predicting the course of contemporary foreign affairs from subtle and forced interpretations of Old Testament writings strikes many as requiring more imagination than writing the script for Star Wars. Certainly the intention and message of these Old Testament Scriptures for the church today cannot be reduced to predicting tomorrow's newspaper headlines.

Further, the ethical implications of this view, if followed consistently, conflict directly with the thrust of the biblical message. If, in fact, things must be worse before they will get better, why try to reverse signs of the world's deterioration? Why work for peace if war is a sign of Christ's coming? Why feed the hungry if we are to expect famine? Why save the creation if its destiny is to be destroyed by fire? As author Tom Sine suggests in *The Mustard Seed Conspiracy,* believing in this vision of the future would have us torpedo the grain boats in order to advance famine and bring us close to the millennium.

Even when the more extreme positions of dispensationalism are rejected, Christians committed to a premillennial view are still faced with the challenge of constructing an ethic motivating Christians to be involved in the task of bringing God's shalom, justice, and peace to the creation, and doing so now, rather than waiting for the end. The more prevalent tendency is for these Christians to withdraw into a counter-cultural enclave that views the "world" as evil and sees little hope of changing its conditions. Notable exceptions can be found, such as theologian Vernon C. Grounds, whose book *Revolution and the Christian Faith* is proof that premillennialists can be passionately concerned for social justice. But voices like his within the premillennial camp remain a minority.

Premillennialism responds exclusively to only one tributary within the stream of the Bible's message. Certainly, some Scriptures picture growing calamity as history draws to a close (for instance, Matthew 24:6-8, Mark 13:7-8, Luke 21:10-11). Other Scriptures, however, underscore that God's Kingdom and reign over creation are already established. In Luke 17:20-21, for example, we read that the Pharisees asked Christ when the kingdom of God will come. Christ replied, "You cannot tell by observation when the kingdom of God comes. There will be no saying. 'Look, here it is!' or 'there it is!'; for in fact the kingdom of God is among you." Christ's teaching and ministry are aimed at announcing the inauguration of the Kingdom of God, which takes a foothold in history in the midst of the present age.

Likewise, the focus of passages such as Colossians 1:13-14 emphasizes that our experience of this kingdom begins not at the end of time, but in our present life. "He rescued us from the domain of darkness and brought us away into the kingdom of his dear Son, in whom our release is secured and our sins forgiven." The epistle then continues, in verses we previously examined, extending this new rulership by Christ over all creation. "His is the primacy over all created things" (1:15). In passages such as these there is no indication that Christ's reconciliation of the whole universe awaits some future date. Rather, the proclamation is that this has already been accomplished. In the same fashion, Paul declares in 2 Corinthians 5:17, "When anyone is united to Christ, there is a new world; the old order has gone, and a new order has already begun."[3]

Is there a theological tradition concerning the future that struggles to preserve this biblical tension? Yes. Traditionally, it has been called amillennialism. On the one hand, this stance recognizes that the promise of God's reign is not merely consigned to the future, but establishes its roots in the present. At the same time, amillennialism recognizes that there is no simple, progressive unfolding of the kingdom. The new order has begun now, but the old order is still present.

Theologians, in describing the coming Kingdom of God, have spoken of the tension between the "already" and the "not yet." This helps to capture the full biblical picture concerning God's redemption of creation. Oscar Cullman has used the wartime analogy of D–Day and V–Day to describe this same truth.[4] Christ's life, death, and resurrection is the triumphant invasion of God's grace, claiming the world as God's own. The final victory, V–Day, is assured, fulfilled at the end of history. The church finds itself in between these two times, in the midst of tension and battle, yet knowing that the triumph inaugurated on D–Day will be complete.

Augustine, along with Luther, Calvin, and most of the Reformers, held to an amillennial view.[5] The thousand years referred to in Revelation 20 is not taken literally, but figuratively, like many of the symbols and references found there. Amillennialism holds that Christ's triumphant reign over creation, acknowledged by the church, has already begun and grows even while forces of rebellion attempt to pull the creation toward destruction and death. The disarming of those rebellious powers is assured by Christ's victory. "On that cross he discarded the cosmic powers and authorities like a garment; he made a public spectacle of them and led them as captives in his triumphal procession" (Colossians 2:15). Yet they do not finally give up their grasp over creation without an ongoing struggle. "For our fight is not against human foes, but against cosmic powers, against authorities and potentates of this dark world" (Ephesians 6:12).

The amillennial perspective recognizes both the creation's blessing as God's gift and the "curse" that falls upon humanity for taking possession of creation as part of the biblical message. Graphically, we can picture this position as follows:

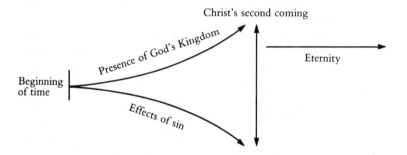

We do well to keep in mind the various ways in which the New Testament refers to the "world," as discussed in the last chapter, when we fashion a biblical view of the future. In one sense, this world—meaning the organization of life apart from God—is rushing toward judgment, and destined to pass away. Yet, God's salvation reaches to this world, and to the whole creation, in order to win it back to God. The destiny of creation is determined not by its rebellion, but finally by its redemption through Jesus Christ.

Even that most apocalyptic passage of the gospel found in Matthew 24 and 25 does not end with an admonition to withdraw from a world headed for destruction. On the contrary, the basis of the final judgment is the extent of one's engagement in the world, feeding the hungry, giving drink to the thirsty, providing shelter to the homeless, clothing the naked, and giving comfort to the imprisoned—in short, re-establishing God's shalom within the creation (Matthew 25:31–46). Christ, who is the prince of this shalom, and present in all creation, is the One who is served by these acts.

In response to signs of potential destruction and calamity within the creation, Jesus calls his followers to concrete actions that claim the creation as God's own, extending God's compassion to heal the wounds of the world. Our salvation, according to this passage, seems dependent on our actions, which testify to God's healing and saving intention for the world. Those who fail to respond hear the words, "The curse is upon you" (25:41). But those who faithfully act to restore creation hear the Son of Man say, "You have my Father's blessing; come, enter, and possess the kingdom that has been ready for you since the world was made" (25:34).

We are still left with questions to answer decisively. How is the creation made different today—if at all—by God's redemption? Is its water purer, its air cleaner, and its earth more productive? The evidence examined in the first chapter suggests the opposite. Does this redemption offer a reprieve from the threat of nuclear destruction? Again, the nuclear arms race increases the probability of nuclear war day by day. If the new creation does not wait for history's end, but already has begun, how is this manifested?

The heart of the distortion that afflicts all creation is the blasphemous rebellion by humanity, which seeks to be god over the creation. The "fall" is not a biological fact, but a fracturing of relationships. Convinced that creation is at its disposal, humanity has attempted to make the creation its slave. Its resources are wantonly squandered, its life-supporting capacity is threatened, and its very existence is endangered. In trying to make creation its slave, humanity subjects itself to the bondage of powers that would claim sovereignty over the world in opposition to God.

Concretely, this means that energy companies rape the northern Great Plains, strip-mining coal. Multinational companies raze the Amazon rainforest, destroying hundreds of species of life as well as endangering the globe's atmosphere in order to graze cattle so that they can export meat to affluent societies. Wastes from industrial plants are discharged both from smoke stacks and sewer pipes in Lake Michigan, depositing four hundred known toxic chemicals into its water and making consumption of many of its fish a hazard to human health.

The creation groans, for it has become subject to humanity's rebellion. Astronauts have looked down from space at this bluish green sphere of life, suspended in the universe, and marveled. Yet, their closer examination reveals dirty-brown blotches, spreading like a cancerous infection. It is the evidence of a civilization attempting to extend its reign over the creation.

But redemption claims the creation as God's. It does so by restoring us in fellowship to God, as God's servants, God's children. Then creation becomes once again God's gift. We relate to creation as the life-endowing gift of grace, flowing from the goodness of the Creator.

This is why creation waits for the revealing of the children of God (Romans 8:19). God's redemption extends to the creation as God restores the relationship between humanity and creation through Jesus Christ. Those incorporated into Christ are called to live out this redeemed relationship to the creation. And in this way, the first fruits and signs of creation's redemption are experienced, here and now.

Granted, these are only signs. Recycling tin cans and glasses seems lacking in cosmic significance. Yet, in the daily, down-to-earth ways of living, we can discover the meaning of receiving creation as a gift and preserving its life out of gratitude and faithfulness to God. Creation experiences the first fruits of its liberation. This is how creation's redemption, assured by Jesus Christ, finds initial expression in the present time.

But what then of creation's ultimate destiny? Does the new creation imply, in the end, a destruction of the old? Does this world pass away in order for the "new heavens and new earth" to appear? Are we asked to preserve what God will eventually destroy?

Some biblical passages, at first reading, suggest such a radical break between the old and new creation. 2 Peter 3:10, for instance, says, "the elements will disintegrate in flames, and the earth with all that is in it will be laid bare" and continues in verse 13, "But we have this promise, and look foward to new heavens and a new earth." Likewise, Revelation 21 speaks of seeing "a new heaven and a new earth, for the first heaven and the first earth had vanished" (21:1). These are the two major New Testament passages suggesting that the new creation entails the destruction of the present creation. But in each case we must ask the purpose of these passages.[6]

The setting of 2 Peter finds opponents arguing that there would be no second coming, which by then already seemed long delayed. Nothing new would happen, and events would continue as in the past. To counter this argument, the epistle sets forth the certainty of Christ's second coming, and the final judgment. Things will not continue as they are. A decisive end will come. This is the point of the passage. "The question of the continuity or discontinuity between the world of creation and the new world is therefore not the aim. . . ."[7]

In Revelation, filled with so much imagery and metaphor, the one line about the first heaven and the first earth vanishing stands in contrast to visions of the earth and its creatures in a renewed, glorified state.

Revelation 5:13 describes this in part as follows: "Then I heard every created thing in heaven and on earth and under the earth and in the sea, all that is in them, saying, 'Praise and honour, glory and might, to him who sits on the throne and to the Lamb forever.' " Revelation 22, describing the new heavens and new earth, states, "Then he showed me the river of the water of life, sparkling like crystal, flowing from the throne of God and of the Lamb, down the middle of the city's street. On either side of the river stood a tree of life, which yields twelve crops of fruit, one for each month of the year; the leaves of the trees serve for the healing of the nations. Every accursed thing shall disappear" (Revelation 22:1–3). The vision recalls creation in Genesis 2, with a river flowing out from Eden to water the four corners of the earth, and a tree of life. Creation is brought back to God, the Alpha and Omega.

In one sense, creation is totally new, unlike anything in our experience. Yet, it is the stuff of this creation that is so radically transformed; the physical material and creatures of this creation, of which we are a part, are made into a new creation, which is beyond our ability to describe rationally.

Passages examined earlier in Isaiah speak of God's redemption as transforming the inner qualities of nature into a perfect harmony even between animals. And the new heavens and new earth of Isaiah 65 and 66 are filled with visions of people living in harmony with the fruitfulness of the earth, and include a mission reaching out to all humanity (Isaiah 66:23).

Thus, the Bible can speak of the world, existing under the mad rule of humanity, as being annihilated. But in the same way, the creation, originally fashioned to be God's, is brought into perfection at the end of time through the creative, saving work of Jesus Christ.

What the Bible asserts most emphatically throughout is that the salvation of the world is wrought by God. Humanity's efforts cannot achieve it. In the end, the new world of creation, fully present with God, is beyond what we can even imagine. This is God's redemptive work.

Yet the Bible also tells us that this new creation begins now, both in our lives and in the whole created order. And just as the redemption of our lives is to promote the work of sanctification, transforming our lives into the life of Christ, so the redemption of the creation should promote works of sanctifying the earth, transforming it through the sovereignty of Christ.

This new creation comes through death and resurrection. The pattern is not a gradual, upward evolutionary ascent to the Omega point. The fallen powers are judged and overcome in order for the new to dawn. Any survey of the contemporary perils facing the creation demonstrates how much of the old—the power of death—must die. But the God who makes all things new does not sit back and delight in watching a cosmic crescendo of evil, and neither should we. God has already begun the new creation, and we are called to this work of global sanctification.

For will not the water that flows from God's throne be like the water that flows through the streams of this earth? Will not the tree of life, bearing its fruit, be something like the trees that give us fruit? Does not the New Jerusalem come down to its home on this earth? So should we not strive to make this present creation ready to receive God's new creation?

The power of God's redemption is demonstrated decisively for all creation in the resurrection of Jesus Christ. The resurrection of Christ's body means emphatically that this world, the stuff of our bodies and of this earthly creation, is transformed, renewed, and fashioned into a new creation through God's power and grace. We are not delivered from this world, nor are we simply assured of a greater spiritual reality lying beyond this world. Rather, the resurrection means that the power of sin and death is defeated, and overcome, in this world, at the heart of the creation.

Our new life in Christ has its roots and bears its first fruits here, within our own broken and mortal lives. Likewise, the new life in Christ for all creation begins here, with this creation, in its brokenness. Moreover, these are not separate spheres of Christ's redemptive activity, as though humanity and nature are disjointed. It is the one activity of restoring all things in the universe into unity with the Creator.

Evangelicals, who have fought the hardest to preserve the truth of the bodily resurrection of Christ as a doctrine, would do well to realize the meaning of this belief for a theology of creation, especially in a time of ecological emergency.

The body of Jesus—the earthly life of the Incarnate Son—triumphed over the power of sin and death, offering the promise of new life to the whole of the created world. Think of John's account of Jesus on the shore, while the disciples are out fishing once again, after the crucifixion. He is on the beach, beside the sea, with a fire, cooking breakfast. The disciples come, and he serves them fish and bread. Earth, water, air, and fire seem integrated, whole, and redeemed. Christ then said to those that loved him, "Follow me."

He invites us all to breakfast with him at the dawn of the new creation.

NOTES

1. A good description of "dispensational premillennialism" and "historic premillennialism" is found in *The Meaning of the Millennium,* Robert G. Clouse, ed. (Downers Grove, Ill.: Inter-Varsity Press, 1977).
2. Vernon Grounds, *Revolution and the Christian Faith* (Philadelphia: J. B. Lippincott, 1971).
3. The most faithful translation of this verse is "there is a new world" (New English Bible) or "new creation" (Revised Standard Version), rather than "he is a new creature." See John Howard Yoder, *The Politics of Jesus* (Grand Rapids, Mich.: Eerdmans, 1972), pp. 226–28.
4. Oscar Cullman, *Christ and Time,* rev. ed. (Philadelphia: The Westminster Press, 1964), p. 84.
5. Clouse, *The Meaning of the Millenium,* p. 10.
6. See, for example, Odil Hannes Steck, *World and Environment* (Nashville: Abingdon, 1980), pp. 256–258, for his brief but cogent discussion of these passages.
7. Ibid., p. 257.

III. THE PROSPECT: CREATION RESTORED

8. Life as Grace

Moments of deep inward spiritual encounter and life-changing commitments have emerged, in my life's journey, during times of retreat. Consistently, during those occasions, I have found the awesome wonder of creation inviting me to open myself, contemplatively, to hidden areas of my life, and then beckon my heart beyond myself to God. Given over to the flow of God's love, I then find myself yearning to respond to God's ongoing redemptive work in the world.

Browsing through my personal journal, I found these words written a decade ago during a few engaging days spent at a Trappist monastery:

On a walk that afternoon as I looked at the trees through the mist and the gray sky beyond it, all covered by a soft, slight rainy air, I gazed, and I sensed that there was a deeper reality behind this all—but a reality that was also present in the creation. I watched my breath condense into small bits of clouds; yes, a deeper reality, transcendent, yet still immanent; involved in the created, visible, sensual order of things, yet transcendent from, and not bound by it; rather upholding it, girding up all that is created. . . .

Later, down by the river, I tried to free a log and push it into the stream, but was unable. But then I found another, thrust it into the river and pushed it out on its way, with two small branches. And I followed, watching as they flowed down the side of the river, passing obstacles, moving on. Liberated. I thought about my vocation. It was like that—to try to remove the barriers and enable liberation. To help break free the flow of love and concern, to free us from a few of those things—institutions, attitudes, laws—that keep people in bondage and potential decay; to see new ways of God's grace flowing to humanity, building new levels of community and creating new openings for love.

During those years, I was working on Capitol Hill in Washington, D.C. Amidst the frantic pace of that life, involvement within the Church of the Saviour was introducing me to the crucial need for nurturing the life of contemplative prayer. Gradually, I began to pry myself free enough from the demands of relevance and work so that space could emerge for this inward journey. Sometimes it took unusual forms. On a solitary trip to Norway, I sat at the Northcape, above the Artic Circle where the sun sets for only a few hours in August, and wrote:

Midnight, at the Northcape, watching for the dawn, waiting for the light of the world. . . . All the cathedrals faced east toward the rising sun, the rising Christ. But there must always be the hopeful waiting. It drizzles outside now; clouds overhead. But the horizon looks clear, discernible in this gray twilight. There is veiled illumination all around, but no sun yet. Just the light after sunset, before sunrise. Hopeful waiting. Expectation. The certainty that the victory is won, that Christ has risen. All has been conquered. And we shall see the evidence once more, and have our faith renewed again. . . .

"These things are written that you might believe . . . and that in that faith you may have life as his disciples." To have life. The horizon is lighter now—not yet with the sun's first rays, but the dusk fades. To have life. Eternal life—a quality of living. To be possessed by love. To know the victory. To grasp the unity, the oneness of it all.

I read from Yoder's *Politics of Jesus* earlier this evening. To receive Christ, and be "in Christ"—this is not just to have some inner existential transformation. It is to apprehend a whole other *external* reality. In the cross and the resurrection, all the divisions, all the enmity, all the hostility, all that separates one from another—that has all been overcome. He died for all. And loves all. His love is victorious. All are one, seen in his love. In Christ, we grasp this new reality. "All things become new."

The first faint indication, in the clouds, of some other light, other than the gray, begins to appear. It is 7:05 A.M. Sunday morning. What does it mean, Lord, for me to have life?

The impulses of the spiritual journey direct me continually toward a letting go, an abandonment. My dreams, my desires, my pride, my willfulness—these are peeled away, always in new incisive ways, like so many layers of an onion. But ultimately, what is abandoned is the perception of myself as the center of existence, with the world's life organized around me. Believing that I am in control and deserve to be, believing that I can chart my own course, and acting as though the world can be molded into a pattern that suits my own inclinations—this is the essential distortion in my thinking, revealed whenever I gave solitude space in my life.

Perhaps I am drawn at those moments to an intimacy with the creation because it so dramatically calls me beyond myself. The fjords and the mountains move me so because they make it impossible to hold onto myself as the center of existence. The framework is changed. "If I lift up my eyes to the hills, where shall I find help? Help comes only from the Lord, maker of heaven and earth" (Psalm 121:1–2).

The wonder of the creation calls us toward the Creator. We are invited outside ourselves, and offered a vision of life with God as its center.

> For the Lord is a great God, a great king over all gods;
> the farthest places of the earth are in his hands,
> and the folds of the hills are his;
> the sea is his, he made it;
> the dry land fashioned by his hands is his.
> Come: Let us throw ourselves at his feet in homage,
> let us kneel before the Lord who made us;
>   for he is our God,
> we are his people, we the flock he shepherds.
>
> (Psalm 95:3–7)

The inspiration we feel in the presence of creation's grandeur causes us to transcend ourselves and move beyond our own lives as the point of reference. This is a testimony to the presence of God in the world. When one is moved beyond a preoccupation with his or her own being to a recognition of the greatness beyond self, when one has an urge for worship and adoration, then one is being moved by God and toward God.

Even John Calvin wrote, "It can be said, reverently, that nature is God."[1] This is not to limit or equate God with the creation, nor to invite a worship of nature. Rather, it underscores that the creation exists in and through God. When we allow ourselves to encounter the full reality of this creation—something modern urbanized society nearly prevents—we are called beyond ourselves, and ultimately beyond just the creation to the Source of all life.

I do not find God in nature. Rather, in my experience, when I am open and present within the creation, God finds me.

It may seem strange to suggest that the initial fruit of a restored awareness of creation's glory is renunciation. Yet, the spiritual journey always incorporates such a giving up and letting go. But what exactly is given up?

The leaders of some movements through the centuries—at times monastic, and at other points fundamentalist—have postulated that the world must be renounced. Confusing the "world" with "sin," they have sought to avoid earthly contamination in their quest for spiritual purity. We have already examined the biblical misinterpretation resulting from this stance. In practice, such lives seem focused on one's individual righteousness. Despite all the rhetoric about surrender, life retains an ironically selfish centering around the person's spiritual state.

Spiritual abandonment calls us to move beyond a life focused on ourselves. The true purpose of the ascetic tradition in monasticism is not to flee the world somehow, but rather to free the individual from the drive to seek security and identity apart from God. This tendency prevents us from seeing the truth about ourselves, distorts our relationship to the world, and removes us from God. The spiritual journey calls us to give up such a life.

In these terms we can understand Thomas Merton when he wrote, "What is important is not liberation from the body but liberation from the mind. We are not entangled in our own body but entangled in our own mind."[2]

The purpose of renunciation is not rejection, but reception. We let go of a false relationship to ourselves, others, the world, and God in order to receive life as the gift of God's grace. Suddenly we are touched by the truth—the life that comes from God, which reaches out to all creation, and which is rooted in the love of God in Jesus Christ.

This truth is not grasped intellectually, as if it were ours to possess. Rather, it comes to us in the emptiness of our abandonment, overwhelming us like a fresh-flowing stream giving nourishment and life to parched land. We are caught up in its flow, and suddenly we sense that our lives and the life of the world exist only to be infused with the love of the Creator.

A new vision of reality dawns in our hearts. Love is at the center of the universe because Christ is there. It propels and drives all life, pushing its way up through cracks and crevices between the rocks of hatred and suffering. Just like the tree whose growth can dislodge boulders, or the lichen whose existence testifies that a cold stone can be overtaken by warm life, the love of Christ perpetually gives life to the world.

This love was fully present in the life of Jesus of Nazareth, God's Son. He revealed, and his disciples demonstrated, that all people could partake in this life. The heart of the universe, the force behind all existence, could flow into the life of an individual. It can invade the fabric of human relationships, creating community. Always it is there, pressing against the forces and structures that divide humanity, inflict oppression and suffering, and nourish war.

At every front, in every life, in every group, in every nation, at any point, the love of Christ—the spiritual power of his life and the source of all creation—can break through and flow, making all things new.

When grasped by this love, we sense its transcendence over all, just as the majesty of the creation calls us to transcend ourselves. But then, there comes almost simultaneously another awareness: the presence, or immanence, of this love to all creation. Moreover, this wonder of creation includes us, but not as individual, isolated selves; rather we are part of the whole sweep and force of creation. Our true selves—the hidden self, as Paul says in Colossians—is one with Christ, who is behind and within all the creation. "He exists before everything, and all things are held together in him" (Colossians 1:17). And we, through union with Christ, participate in this realm of existence. Our true identity is rooted in a oneness with Christ, and through him with all creation. His love includes us in its redeeming embrace of the creation. United to Christ, we can pour out our lives for the sake of the world, knowing that nothing "can separate us from the love of God in Jesus Christ our Lord" (Romans 8:39).

Our relationship to the creation, then, is transformed by the intersection of God's love in our lives. Thus our task is not, fundamentally, to raise our consciousness, or become more educated and aware, or to be politicized, or to become ecologically sensitive. All those things have their separate and important place. But the beginning point is a spiritual process that roots our lives in God's love rather than self-love.

This spirituality does not operate separately from the concrete dimensions of our relationship to creation, including the realities of hunger, injustice, and war. Rather, it is at the heart of those relationships. Our response is part of this spiritual transformation.

We see such an integrated spirituality evident in the life of St. Francis of Assisi. His extreme poverty was merely the means for his openness to God, and to God's creation. What resounds in Francis's life is not a frightful retreat from the world, but rather a transforming engagement with all creation. In emptying himself, he was overwhelmed in his inmost being with the wonder of God's love, which united him to all creation. Through this experience of the heart, he wrote and sang "The Song of the Creatures":

> Most high and most holy, most powerful Lord,
>   Whom with honor and blessing and praise we acclaim,
> No man can be worthy to utter the word,
>   The Name of thy Name!
>
> To Thee and thy creatures we proffer our praise:
>   To our brother the Sun in the heavens ashine,
> Who brings us the beauty and joy of our days,
>   Thy emblem and sign.

We praise thee, O Lord, for our sister the moon,
    For the stars of the night shining sweetly together,
For our brother the wind, for the bright of the noon,
    For all thy weather.

For our sister the water, so humble and chaste,
    For beautiful fire, with his perilous powers,
For our mother the earth, who holds us embraced,
    Who delights us with flowers.[3]

And whether or not his preaching to the birds is apocryphal, St. Francis demonstrated how all creation becomes new to the person who is in Christ.

Similarly, Benedictine monasteries demonstrated the union of spirituality with a new vision of creation. Although they differed from the Franciscans in stressing the transformation of nature rather than a simple openness to the creation, Benedictine monasteries were often models in the Middle Ages of a restored and fruitful relationship between humanity and creation. One task of the monastery was to cultivate its grounds, which were usually in remote locations, into abundant gardens and fields. These patches of creation, in their view, were being won back to God, and this was a part of their spiritual calling.

Our churches today are afflicted either with a piety which eschews the world, or a worldliness which shuns piety. We stand in need of Christian spirituality, which genuinely reconnects us to God, the whole creation, and one another. At the end of his classic, *New Seeds of Contemplation,* Thomas Merton offers this glimpse of what that might involve:

The Lord plays and diverts Himself in the garden of His creation, and if we could let go of our own obsession with what we think is the meaning of it all, we might be able to hear His call and follow Him in His mysterious, cosmic dance. We do not have to go very far to catch the echoes of that game, and of that dancing. When we are alone on a starlit night; when by chance we see the migrating birds in autumn descending on a grove of junipers to rest and eat; when we see children in a moment when they are really children; when we know love in our own hearts; or when, like the Japanese poet Basho we hear an old frog land in a quiet pond with a solitary splash—at such times the awakening, the turning inside out of all values, the "newness," the emptiness and the purity of vision that make themselves evident, provide a glimpse of the cosmic dance. For the world and time are the dance of the Lord in emptiness. . . . We are in the midst of it, and it is in the midst of us, for it beats in our very blood, whether we want it to or not.[4]

Modern humanity desecrates the creation so drastically and blithely because its corporate life is spiritually impoverished. Society scoffs at any vision which binds together God, humanity, and creation. Instead, God is confined to the realm of the "sacred" and severed from the "profane" world of creation. The division takes many forms, both within and without the church. Theologically, the supernatural is contrasted to the natural. It is normally alleged that the creation functions according to the dictates of laws designed by God, but obeyed by the "natural" world that functions quite adequately on its own. But on some "miraculous" occasions, God's supernatural intervention overturns those natural laws with spectacular results.

Legally, society speaks of a division between church and state, and assumes that spiritual convictions can be confined to the personal realm and kept separate from politics and education. In countless ways our society strives to keep God in his place.

This separation of the "spiritual" from the "natural," and the relegation of God to an innocuous, private compartment of life is directly relevant to the ecological, technological, and nuclear threats to the world. We speak of these threats as though they were simply a result of humanity's shortsightedness. Actually, they are the final result of treating the world as simply a thing unto itself, severing it from God like the fruit first grasped from the tree in the garden.

Christian faith can respond first by nurturing a biblical vision that does not recognize a dichotomy between the sacred and the secular. Life must be grasped in its wholeness once again through the work of God's spirit in our hearts. Then we will have a saving and redeeming witness to offer to the world.

Our restored relationship to the creation is discovered and nurtured first of all in the life of prayer. In such prayer, we open ourselves to the presence of God. The veil of our self-sufficiency is lifted. The hold on our mind of countless preoccupations is temporarily broken. We let go of our defenses. Gradually, we shed our layers of protectiveness like the casings of a mayfly; these layers may have guarded us, and even nurtured us, but now they must fall away if the purpose for which we were born—an upward ascent in the open air—is to be realized.

The mayfly lives most of its life at the bottom of a stream, surrounded by a covering of debris that it has fashioned into a protective shell. That is its world—clinging to rocks in a streambed on the inside of a shell. But when it is beckoned toward transformation, it moves in its nymphal form out of its shelter, beginning its promising but risky journey toward the water's surface. And then, with newly discovered wings dried by the sun, it lifts toward the sky; suddenly its days are filled with activity, energy, and purpose of a life lived on a whole new level of experience.

What has happened is not just that the mayfly has been transformed. Rather, from the perspective of the mayfly, the whole creation has become new. Its inner transformation has apparently led to the outer re-creation of the world.

Of course the air, the trees, and the sky above the water were always there. In one sense, nothing in creation really has changed except the mayfly. But for the mayfly, life outside of its casing and above the water simply did not exist. And in its journey of abandonment and rebirth, the whole creation becomes new.

That is how prayer is to function in our lives. The abandonment of those exterior shells of self-centered security and identity leaves us vulnerable to God. And this vulnerability enables God's spirit to affect our inner transformation. Beckoned on our journey toward God, more than our lives are made new. Rather, a whole new creation opens up to our experience. The world bursts forth as God's gift, resplendent as a sign of God's life. Our union with this new life draws us not away from the world, but rather carries us into the heart of creation. In prayer, all things become new, and we are thrust into an engagement with the world as the fruit of our contemplation.

During the Saturday night resurrection vigil at Orthodox churches, the congregation sings, "for, through the Cross, joy came into the whole world." Christ's journey to the cross was his ultimate act of abandonment and submission. He was totally humble and vulnerable, emptying himself in death on the cross. In that emptiness, he even cried, "My God, my God, why hast thou forsaken me?" (Matthew 27:46). And yet he declared in trusting faithfulness, "Father, into thy hands I commit my spirit" (Luke 23:46).

Through this letting go, this pouring out of his life, salvation and joy break into the whole world. For this becomes the occasion for God's gift of resurrection and new life, the basis of all joy. As Alexander Schmemann writes in *For the Life of the World.*

This joy is pure joy because it does not depend on anything in this world, and is not the reward of anything in us. It is totally and absolutely a *gift,* the *charis,* the grace. And being pure gift, this joy has a transforming power, *the only really transforming power in this world.* . . . Joy was given to the church *for the world*—that the church might be a witness to it and transform the world by joy.[5]

Christ's abandonment on the cross opened the way for his resurrection, and then sent his followers as Christ's body into mission to the whole world. So, likewise, the prayerful giving over of our lives to God imparts to us the gift of resurrected life, and sends us into the world with a transforming vision and mission. Once we are truly in God's hands, rather than in the secure shell of a righteous piety, we will find ourselves present in a new way to both the groaning and the glory of creation.

In Christ we are one with the Prince of Shalom, who breaks every bond of oppression. Because we know that Christ's redeeming power reaches to all the creation, we are thrust into the midst of the world's suffering, darkness, and evil.

Today, a simple exposure to the media's coverage of world

events can overwhelm us with the pervasiveness of sin's power and apparent domination. We are presented with the picture of a world on the brink of actual self-destruction, gripped by nationalistic pride and international phobia. Poverty torments the lives of millions, in full view of the squandering luxury of a few. And the defilement of the earth itself seems to spread like a mortal infection.

Yet, our engagement with the world should not spring forth simply as a response to these realities. Rather our encounter with the world is rooted in Christ's redeeming wounds. Because we have first grasped the world as redeemed, we can meet the world's desperate brokenness with a witness of restoring love. "Because we have first seen the beauty of the world, we can now see the ugliness."[6]

The New Testament Greek word for joy is "chara." Its root is the same as the Greek word for grace, "charis." All joy is possible only because of grace. But what is the meaning of grace?

Originally, the term referred to the qualities of radiance or charm—what we sometimes call gracefulness—in a person. As this charm flowed out, it naturally attracted a response from others. Love radiated back to the source of grace. Thus, grace consists of this relationship of beckoning attraction and love.[7]

By reducing grace to a theological doctrine, we can miss its basic qualities. Grace begins with the Creator—a point constantly reaffirmed by theology. But in life, what this means is that an attracting love radiates out from God to the creation, imparting life itself. As Merton says, "Grace is life."[8] This grace flows out to every person. In spite of the sin and willful separation from God, and in spite of the person's nothingness before God, this grace loves, accepts, and attracts a response back to the Creator.

What makes the person lovely, beautiful, and acceptable to God is simply this grace. The life it gives—both the simple physical life, and the spiritual aliveness—is God's gift. So the source of our joy, and of our sense of being worthy, lovable people, comes not from ourselves, but from God. The grace that radiated to us from God can be reflected back from us to God. Our spiritual journey consists of opening our lives in ever new ways to make them clearer channels for the flow of this grace.

But this grace does not simply extend to people. It flows out to all the creation. Our failure to see this truth has fostered a truncated view of grace, as though it were simply part of the formula for our salvation rather than the heart of life for ourselves and all creation.

The beauty and radiance of the creation resides not simply in itself, but rather in its relationship to God. Here is where Christianity distinguishes itself from various forms of animism and pantheism. All life in creation exists only because of God. Its glory and majesty is simply the occasion for creation to reflect grace back to God. Just as a person becomes lovely in God's eyes as he or she receives God's grace, so all creation is being transformed through the radiance of God's grace.

"Charis" is also the root for the word charity. Its original meaning referred to the love of God. The response to such grace, or love, is deep gratitude. This is far more than simply being thankful. Rather, such gratitude re-orients all of life. We live no longer on the basis of what we have done or who we are, but rather from the foundation of what we have received from God through Christ. Now we can reflect this same love to others, to all creation, and back to God. And our gratitude finds expression, first of all, through our worship and praise.

The heart of that worship is communion, or the Eucharist. This word as well takes its root from "charis." The Eucharist is the feast of thanksgiving. In it, this transforming grace comes to us, as God's people, and radiates through us.

As God's gift to us, the Eucharist both commemorates the redemptive work of Jesus Christ and is the means, or sacrament, for that grace to continually touch our lives. Through its celebration, we become open once again to receive this gift, or this "charisma." Such reception is not mere acknowledgement, but rather the partaking of this life into our most inner being. We become charismatic people, filled with this grace.

Much of the Protestant tradition, in its desire to avoid viewing the communion table as a spiritual gas tank, has emphasized the

Eucharist only as a commemorative event—much like a memorial service—with a purely individualistic focus. In some Reformed liturgies, those in the congregation are asked the week before the infrequent celebration of communion to prepare their hearts. The communion liturgy itself contains an almost exclusively personal focus; the act is strictly an individual's commemoration of his or her own salvation through Christ. The individualized miniature glass cups and pre-cut pieces of bread that are passed to each person in the pew reinforces this sense. Three hundred private little communion services seem to be going on, rather than a single service where the community as one celebrates the foundation of its life together.

As the sacrament of God's grace, the Eucharist is not limited in its focus to individuals. Other Christian traditions have been more attentive both to the corporate dimensions of the Eucharist and to its celebration of grace, which extends to all creation.

The traditional Eucharist celebration begins as the bread and wine, along with the offerings of the congregation, are brought to the communion table. All these are gifts from God, and they are now being brought back to God. The bread and wine taken from the fields and cultivated by "the work of human hands" are the most basic of God's gifts to us. When Christ first took the bread and the cup of wine that evening, he offered thanks to God his Father, acknowledging again that all provision for life in creation comes to us through the graciousness of God.

In the Eucharistic liturgy, the "preface," or beginning prayer, is climaxed by the ancient hymn, "Holy, holy, holy, God of power and might. Heaven and earth are full of your glory. Hosanna in the highest. Blessed is he who comes in the name of the Lord." The priest often continues, "All creation gives you praise." One Lutheran version puts it this way: "You have filled all creation with light and life: everything everywhere is full of your glory." Clearly, the Eucharist is introducing us into a new vision of all creation. Here, at the communion table, we are present to the joy and life of all the world. As Alexander Schmemann puts it, "In and through this Eucharist the whole creation becomes what it always was to be and yet failed to be."[9]

The priest or minister then takes the bread and the cup, as Christ did, and offers it up to God. These then become the body and blood of Christ. While theologians have debated for centuries what actually happens, one unifying meaning should be clear. These elements of creation provide the occasion for us to partake more deeply in Christ's life. They underscore that just as God's grace provides the simple provision of daily bread for sustaining our life, so this grace infuses us with the bread of life and the cup of blessing.

We take in this life, and are filled with a bread that was broken, and a wine that was poured out. By its very nature, the gift of grace we receive cannot be treasured and held within our own selves. For this "charis" is the life that has won the victory for all the creation. As one communion hymn resounds, "This is the feast of victory for our God, for the Lamb who was slain has begun his reign. Alleluia . . . sing with all the people of God and join in the hymn of all creation: 'Blessing, honor, glory and might be to God and the Lamb forever. Amen.' "

The victory has been won. Creation has been restored. And the reign of Christ has begun. The grace we have received frees and beckons us to the pouring out of our lives for the sake of this reign in all creation. This is the true fruit of our gratitude, and the result of our Eucharistic celebration.

The most powerful example of such a eucharistic way of life I have encountered is the life of the Sisters of Charity, headed by Mother Teresa and begun in Calcutta. During a visit there, what most overwhelmed me was not the sacrificial service given at the Home for the Destitute and the Dying. Rather, it was a room filled with 275 Sisters gathering at 5:30 each morning for worship, prayer, and the Eucharist.

Outside on Lower Circular Road, a stream of humanity struggles to find its way through another day, with needs so desperate that one feels immobilized. But in the convent's chapel, a eucharistic vision of life in Calcutta is nurtured each morning in the hearts of these Sisters.

Following communion the morning I visited, the Sisters recited the prayer of Cardinal Newman:

Dear Jesus, help me to spread thy fragrance everywhere I go. Flood my soul with Thy spirit and life. Penetrate and possess my whole being so utterly that all my life may only be a radiance of Thine. Shine through me and be so in me that every soul I come in contact with may feel Thy presence in my soul. Let them look up and see no longer me but only Jesus! Stay with me, and then I shall begin to shine as Thou shinest, so to shine as to be a light to others; the light, O Jesus, will be all from Thee; none of it will be mine, it will be Thou shining on others through me. Let us thus praise Thee in the way Thou dost love best by shining on those around me. Let me preach Thee without preaching, not by words but by example, by the catching force of the sympathetic influence of what I do, the evident fullness of the love my heart bears to Thee. Amen. [10]

And then they left, prepared to serve the destitute, the hungry, and the dying another day.

For these Sisters, creation has been transformed, now revealing the presence and suffering of Christ. Mother Teresa points to the way the priest holds the bread, consecrated as the Body of Christ, and says, "This is how you should handle the same Body of Christ in the suffering bodies of men." [11] A volunteer who worked with the Sisters of Charity for five months wrote:

This is the real reason why they give themselves completely to tend the body of man, even in its most ravaged state; it is these same bodies, these same arms, these same emaciated legs, this same chest almost lacking the power to breathe, this same spent look, all of these form the throne of the majesty of God. They believe and they understand clearly why Jesus was truly man, flesh of our flesh, blood of our blood, and this same Jesus is still alive today. [12]

In the Eucharist all creation, even its worst agony, is transformed through the presence of God's grace. Entering into the life of Christ in this way is the only means for us to embrace the pain and brokenness of the world with the grace that draws creation back to God. Just as the bread and the wine are brought forth from the creation to become the offering of this eucharistic celebration, so we depart the Eucharist as vessels ready to restore the creation as God's own, offering it back up to God.

We become, it can be said, the "priests of creation." The estrangement of the world from its Creator came through humanity's desire to be its own god. But through Christ the power of this sin has been broken. We who are in Christ can become the mediators of creation. God's redemption of the world calls us to a ministry of global sanctification. Acting to restore the creation and to fulfill God's shalom, the world can be touched ever more deeply with the presence of God's grace. As we celebrate Christ's broken body and poured-out blood, we then embrace the world even as He did:

There must be someone in this world—which rejected God and in this rejection, in this blasphemy, became a chaos of darkness—there must be someone to stand in its center, and to discern, to see it again as full of divine riches, as the cup full of life and joy, as beauty and wisdom, and to thank God for it. This "someone" is Christ, the new Adam, who restores that "eucharistic life" which I, the old Adam, have rejected and lost; who makes me again what I am, and restores the world to me. And if the church *is in Christ,* its initial act is always this act of thanksgiving, of returning the world to God.[13]

NOTES

1. *Calvin: Institutes of the Christian Religion,* John T. McNeill, ed. (Philadelphia: The Westminster Press, 1960), *Institutes* I.v.v., p. 58.
2. Thomas Merton, *The Asian Journal of Thomas Merton* (New York: New Directions Publishing Company, 1973), p. 90.
3. Morris Bishop, *St. Francis of Assisi* (Boston: Little, Brown, and Company, 1974), p. 181.
4. Thomas Merton, *New Seeds of Contemplation* (New York: New Directions Publishing Company, 1961), pp. 296–297.
5. Alexander Schmemann, *For the Life of the World* (St. Vladimir's Seminary Press, 1973), p. 55.
6. Ibid., p. 61.
7. These reflections on grace are enriched by Thomas Merton's words from a series of tape-recorded talks he gave titled "Merton on Life," and in particular the tape titled "Life and Grace."
8. Ibid.
9. Schmemann, *Life of the World,* p. 38.
10. From Missionaries of Charity's *Prayer Book* (Ranchi, India: The Catholic Press), pp. 11–12.
11. From a pamphlet provided by the Missionaries of Charity titled "Choosing to Serve the Destitute," by Paul Chetwti, S.J., p. 11.
12. Ibid.
13. Schmemann, *Life of the World,* pp. 60–61.

9. Creation's Pentecost

The power of God in Jesus Christ to reclaim the creation is a gift to the church. This is the meaning of Pentecost. The Spirit of God, fully present in the person of Jesus Christ, now descends on the church, which becomes Christ's body. God's creative, restoring, and saving power is now present within the corporate life of God's people.

Recent emphasis on the work of the Holy Spirit, underscored for the church by the charismatic movement of the last two decades, has often focused on the gift of the Spirit in the Book of Acts, and its functioning within the life of the New Testament Church. Beyond question, in past years the church—mainline Protestant, Catholic, and evangelical—had neglected the fresh and stirring presence of the Holy Spirit so evident in the early church, and so absent in its own life.

The charismatic movement has now infiltrated broadly into most branches of the church, restoring at least new openness to the work of the Spirit. But in this emphasis, the focus has at times been narrowed to individual renewal and confined to the New Testament.

The charistmatic renewal had its initial modern impact through individuals receiving the baptism of the Spirit, and usually speaking in tongues. The spiritual lives of these Christians were revolutionized. Suddenly, God's Spirit was directly present to them in new and powerful ways. Praying in tongues, or in the Spirit, brought deep blessing and spiritual strength.

The supernatural dimensions of the Christian life took on a whole new power. "Spiritual warfare" became real personal combat. The "enemy" was no mere symbol of evil, but an alive and active spiritual presence attempting to thwart the steadfastness of believers. Increased sensitivity to the Holy Spirit aroused an awareness of evil, demonic spirits.

Ministries of deliverence sprang up, perceiving various personality disorders, illness, or other afflictions as signs of possession by the dark powers of Satan. The response was to pray for deliverance from these forces through the Holy Spirit, in the name of Jesus.

Belief in the power of spiritual healing also grew. From famous television faith healers to quiet but intense prayers for healing in charismatic prayer groups, believers began to trust that God's miraculous powers were present today through the Spirit in their lives.

Yet, that was where the focus often began and ended—the inward life of the believer. The Spirit came individually; its fruits were purely personal. One now possessed new spiritual gifts, such as speaking in tongues. And the work of the Spirit was centered in one's own life, or in the individual life of someone else. The combat between God's Spirit and the "powers and principalities" took place within the lives of people. A common emphasis of influential books in the charismatic movement during that time is demonstrated by the title of Dennis and Rita Bennett's *The Holy Spirit and You*.[1]

This individualized focus on the work of the Holy Spirit bypasses the thrust of the New Testament witness. The outpouring of the Spirit at Pentecost came not to isolated persons, but to the gathered community. The Spirit was given foremost not to single believers, but to the life of the Body of Christ.

Further, the gifts of the Spirit received by specific people were not for their own edification, but rather, for equipping and building up the church. The context for both receiving and exercising such gifts in the New Testament is the corporate, gathered-together Body of Christ.

Of course, the pouring out of the Spirit results in the personal spiritual renewal of believers. That is one of the fruits. But it is not the main function of the Holy Spirit. Rather, such personal renewal is only a part of the renewal in relationships of people knit together as a community of faith. The work of the Holy Spirit is to create and enliven the common life of the church, and to empower that community in its renewing mission to the whole creation.

Several influential figures in the charismatic movement grasped the New Testament emphasis on the Spirit's building of community. One of them was Graham Pulkingham, whose leadership in the Church of the Redeemer at Houston, Texas, was used to transform that Episcopal parish into a vibrant charismatic community during the 1960s. Lives, possessions, and homes were shared, leading to a process of communal transformation. Pulkingham's first book, *Gathered for Power*,[2] described this charismatic journey into community. The sequel, *They Left Their Nets*,[3] documented the parish's ministry to the poor, inner-city neighborhood where the church was located and where its community households sprang up.

The witness in the New Testament of the church after Pentecost sharing all things in common, discovering a unity through following Christ in laying down their lives for one another, and being empowered for mission, all became incarnated at Church of the Redeemer during that time. Pulkingham often commented on how the New Testament came alive in a new way in the context of living life in Christian community.

The legacy of Pulkingham and Church of the Redeemer spread like its creative, worshipful music into the lives of countless new Christian communities over the next decade. Some elements of the charismatic movement began focusing more concretely on community as the work of the Spirit. Other Christians caught by the biblical vision of community looked to the Church of the Redeemer's experience as an instructive and encouraging model.

The Sojourners Community in Washington, D.C., was touched in its early days by Pulkingham's ministry. Jim Wallis and Bob and Jackie Sabath shared deeply with Pulkingham before moving together to Washington, D.C., to begin a community there almost a decade ago. For them, prophetic witness and radical discipleship became anchored in the life of Christian community and worship. The pastoral and the prophetic were deeply united. Sojourners fellowship and its magazine blossomed.

Father Richard Rohr, a Franciscan priest in Cincinnati, experienced an outpouring of the Spirit and started a ministry of teaching and prayer meetings in 1971 that were eventually drawing a thousand people. By the end of 1975 this New Jerusalem prayer group opted for intentional community. Those committed moved into the Winston Place neighborhood of Cincinnati, and others returned to their parishes. An article in *Cincinnati* magazine about the New Jerusalem community said this:

> For Father Rohr, the Spirit's most basic gift is community: the linkage of one believer to another in the Body of Christ. That changes the charismatic ball game because it stresses lifestyle rather than gifts—rather than, say, the praying in tongues. . . .
>
> That sense of community is also at the heart of the appeal of New Jerusalem, and you can ask (someone) what drew him: "People loved me."[4]

Since "charismatic" means being full of the gifts of God's love, it makes sense that communities like New Jerusalem are characterized by an abundance of such grace and love. Likewise, this is why such renewal communities discover the Eucharist to be so central and find worship to be the organic expression and celebration of their life together. They are experiencing together a taste of the new creation in Christ.

Pentecost means that the love and grace present in Jesus Christ are given to his Body, the church. Yet that is not all. Concentrating our attention only on the New Testament account after Pentecost also restricts the biblical interpretation of the Holy Spirit.

This Spirit was present at creation. For before the Spirit blew like a wind through that house at Pentecost to create the church, that Spirit hovered and "swept over the surface of the waters" (Genesis 1:2) to create the world. The Hebrew word for God's spirit, "ruah," is also the word for wind, and wind is consistently used as a metaphor in the Bible for understanding the Spirit. For example, Jesus told Nicodemus that the Spirit is like the wind.

Thus a natural part of creation—wind—is used by the Bible to represent the Spirit, both in the Old and New Testaments. Both at creation and at Pentecost, the presence of the Spirit comes with the blowing of the wind.

The Spirit's initial work was expressed in the fashioning of creation. In addition to blowing over the waters at creation, the Spirit breathed life into the creation ("ruah" also means the "breath," which is the life force of both animals and humans). Thus Job says, "The Spirit of God made me, and the breath of the Almighty gave me life" (Job 33:4).

The Spirit not only creates, but also sustains and renews all life. Psalm 104:30 reads, "You give breath, fresh life begins, you keep renewing the world" (New Jerusalem Bible). Other translations say, "Thou dost send forth Thy Spirit, they are created; And Thou dost renew the face of the ground" (New American Standard Bible, very similar to King James Version). The Spirit gives life not only to the church, but to all creation.

On the day of Pentecost, Peter began his sermon quoting the prophet Joel about the pouring out of God's Spirit on sons and daughters (Acts 2:17). The passage comes from Joel 2:28–32. In Joel's prophecy, right before the verses quoted in Acts, we read this:

> Earth, be not afraid, rejoice and be glad;
> for the Lord himself has done a proud deed.
> Be not afraid, you cattle in the field;
> for the pastures shall be green,
> the trees shall bear fruit,
> the fig and the vine yield their harvest.
> O people of Zion,
> rejoice and be glad in the Lord your God,
> who gives you good food in due measure
> and sends down rain as of old.
> The threshing-floors shall be heaped with grain,
> the vats overflow with new wine and oil.
> (Joel 2:21–24)

The biblical promise of shalom echoed when the Spirit was poured out at Pentecost. God's Spirit was doing more than creating a new people. That Spirit was establishing a new relationship between this people and the creation. Together, this was an expression of the new creation.

The description in Acts attests to this reality. This fellowship met constantly "to share the common life, to break bread, and to pray" (2:42). "All whose faith had drawn them together held everything in common; they would sell their property and possessions and make a general distribution as the need of each required. With one mind they kept up their daily attendance at the temple, and, breaking bread in private houses, they shared their meals together with unaffected joy, as they praised God" (Acts 2:44–47).

Creation had become God's gift once again. All life was given by God's grace, including their life together. Their response was joy, worship, and thanksgiving. Receiving creation as grace freed them to share all with one another.

Pentecost almost immediately brought the church into conflict with the political and religious authorities. Peter and John healed a cripple at the gate of the temple. To the astonished people, Peter proclaimed that the power of Jesus, whom God raised from the dead, had healed the forty-year-old man. The message was clear. God's power had restored Jesus to life. He is the Messiah. His power, present through God's Spirit, has healed the cripple. This was but another sign that they were to expect "the time of universal restoration" (Acts 3:21).

Peter and John were arrested and imprisoned. They were told to stop preaching and teaching, but refused. When they were released, Peter and John rejoined their fellowship. Together the church proclaimed,

Sovereign Lord, maker of heaven and earth and sea and of everything in them, who by the Holy Spirit, through the mouth of David thy servant didst say, "Why did the Gentiles rage and the peoples lay their plots in vain? The kings of the earth took their stand and the rulers made common cause against the Lord and against his Messiah" (Acts 4:24–26).

The conflict ultimately concerned who ruled over the creation. That is always the heart of the church's conflict with the powers of the world. Who rules? Who owns? Who is truly sovereign? And the response of the Spirit-filled church was to declare God's sovereignty over the creation as its Creator. The young church recognized that the "kings of the earth" and those with power would conspire against them as they had against Christ.

The outpouring of the Spirit at Pentecost not only filled the church, but reaffirmed God's rule over all creation—a rule won by the life, death, and resurrection of Jesus Christ. And the church responded, recognizing the threat it posed to the powers that be, but trusting in the power of God's Spirit. The Acts account continues, "When they had ended their prayer, the building where they were assembled rocked, and all were filled with the Holy Spirit and spoke the word of God with boldness. The whole body of believers was united in heart and soul. Not a man of them claimed any of his possessions as his own, but everything was held in common, while the apostles bore witness with great power to the resurrection of the Lord Jesus" (Acts 4:31–33).

The acts of healing following Pentecost were signs that the power of Christ's ministry on earth was being continued through his Body. Just as the healing acts of Jesus were signs of creation being restored, so the healing ministry of the early church was a testimony to the work of the Spirit in proclaiming God's reign.

Christ's resurrection and the signs of healing present with his followers point to the time when all creation will "enter upon the liberty and splendour of the children of God" (Romans 8:21). The Spirit's work and the church's mission reaches out, therefore, to the whole created order. It is no wonder, then, that this first healing in Acts, combined with the proclamation of Christ's resurrection, resulted in Peter and John being arrested and jailed.

The global reach of the Spirit at Pentecost is also evident in the gift of tongues, which enabled preaching in other languages. The comparison to the story of the tower of Babel in Genesis is compelling. Again, wanting to claim godly powers over creation, humanity attempted to build "a city and a tower with its top in the heavens, and make a name for ourselves" (Genesis 11:4). But the Lord confused their language and dispersed them.

At Pentecost, however, Christ's lordship over the creation restores the unity of humanity. The gift of tongues initially experienced by the church was for testifying that the divisions between
cultures were overcome through the restoring work of God's
Spirit.

This work of the Spirit in building the Body of Christ and proclaiming Christ's lordship over creation raises the question of the
church's relationship to the world. Christians have answered that
question, both today and through the ages, in a variety of ways.
We can try to summarize them as follows:

Withdrawing from the world. We have already noted the tendency
of some Christians to flee from any concrete relationships with
society in order to seek their own spiritual purity. Often this is
combined with an apocalyptic mentality, which views all creation
as evil, expects it to be destroyed, and believes that God will save
the souls of a righteous remnant, creating *ex nihilo* a new life in
eternity for them.

Blessing the world as it is. Often called the Constantinian stance,
this response largely accepts the cultural norms, social structures,
and political powers as parts of God's created order. Despite the
fall, these parts of the good creation are providentially ordained
and deserve the church's blessing, support, and involvement. At
times this stance suggests that God's creative activity is now solely
in humanity's hands. God depends on the church to uphold these
orders of creation, such as the state.

Confronting the world with prophetic witness. The fall has fully obscured and defiled the original goodness of creation. Its structures
are fallen, dominated by the principalities and powers. No hope is
found in the world. Rather, as Karl Barth insisted, hope comes
only from the outside. Thus, God's word comes over against the
world. As the community of faith, the church models this stance,
issuing prophetic witness and serving as an iconoclastic challenge
to the world's false sense of security.

Reclaiming the world as God's creation. This option recognizes the
fallen principalities and powers that have dominion in the world,
yet asserts that Christ's victory over them means their terrain can

be, in part, won back. The church is called to an engagement with the world that not only witnesses to it, but also seeks to re-orient and restore its life under Christ's lordship. While only partial signs of success are possible, the church trusts that God's redemption of the creation can begin to make a difference in the present world.

Any summary such as this contains inadequacies and distortions. The point is to simply help us clarify how the church and the world might relate. Further, no one option, it seems to me, is correct at all times historically or holds true for every point where the church and the world meet.

But we can draw some general conclusions. The extremes of withdrawing from the world because it is evil or blessing the world uncritically as good both seem to omit central biblical insights. The Bible affirms that the creation is good, yet recognizes that humanity has distorted its relationship to God and the creation.

Sorting out the third and fourth options in practice is more difficult. Two questions are helpful in clarifying these choices. First, is God's redemptive work in the world expressed primarily through the shape of the church?

John Howard Yoder is the modern theologian most responsible for urging Christians to make the nature of the church itself the focal point for its engagement with the world. He declares that "the primary social structure through which the gospel works to change other structures is that of the Christian community."[5] The church's task is to break free from the seduction of the powers and principalities in order to display to society the lordship of Christ. "The church must be a sample of the kind of humanity within which, for example, economic and racial differences are surmounted. Only then will she have anything to say to the society that surrounds her about how those differences must be dealt with."[6]

The church's relationship to the world must always be grounded in its own lived-out experience of God's redemption. The differences Christians might make in the world begin with the church being different.

Yoder's influential study *The Politics of Jesus* has often been criticized as advising withdrawal from responsible political power. While Yoder does argue that in some situations such a withdrawal is necessary, his point is that certain acts of withdrawal may be another form of intervention within the world.[7] Refusal to work on a defense contract for nuclear missiles or resigning in protest from an enfeebled Environmental Protection Agency would be examples.

Confronting the world with prophetic witness can turn into wholesale withdrawal from the world. But it need not when such witness is made in light of Christ's redemptive victory for all creation. This victory is the foundation of the church's relationship with the world. As Yoder says of the church,

Her calling is to be the conscience and the servant within human society. The church must be sufficiently experienced to be able to discern when and where and how God is using the Powers, whether this be thanks to the faithful testimony of the church or in spite of her infidelity. Either way, she is called to contribute to the creation of structures more worthy of man.[8]

The prophetic witness of the church to the world on various issues is always needed in any time. Believing otherwise assumes either that God's rule over creation is fully realized, or that God's redemptive work is not relevant to the creation. Nevertheless, the church's relationship to the world should not be solely defined by a posture of prophetic resistance.

God's purposes in history are advanced not simply through the calling of a people to obedience, but through reclaiming creation as obedient. The church is primary, for creation begins to experience its restoration not because of some divine fiat, but through the concrete response of humanity. However, the church itself is not the exclusive means nor end of God's work.

The power of God in Jesus Christ has acted to reclaim all creation. The church is called neither to a life in and for itself, nor to treat the creation chiefly as its antagonist. Rather, the community of faith is to be the vessel through which the life of Jesus Christ can take on flesh and bones today, extending God's love to the whole created world. The grace of Jesus Christ and the power of the Holy Spirit calls the church into being for the sake of the whole world's life.

Alexander Schmemann expresses this truth cogently when discussing baptism and ecclesiology, the doctrine of the church:

> But ecclesiology, unless it is given its true cosmic perspective ("for the life of the world"), unless it is understood as the Christian form of "cosmology," is always ecclesiolatry, the Church considered as a "being in itself" and not the new relation of God, man, and the world.[9]

This brings us to the second clarifying question: Does this new order of creation begin now, both for the church and the world?

If the new creation begins only after the end of history, and if a wall between then and now cannot be crossed over from either side, even for a scant glance, then we are consigned either to withdraw from the world, or to resist the world with acts of defiant witness. But the victory of Jesus Christ has opened up the world to the power of God's redemption. This is the persistent claim of the Bible.

Once we grasp that the scope of God's activity is truly cosmic, and that God's work of creation through Jesus Christ will be brought to its fulfillment, then the church's relationship to the world reflects redemption rather than merely resistance.

But here too there is a danger. The desire to reclaim the world as God's can turn into the attitude of blessing the world as it is. But it need not as long as we remember that this redemption came through death on the cross, and that the powers that crucified the Lord of creation continue their fight to keep the world in their grasp.

The testimony of the New Testament is that these fallen powers and principalities are disarmed and redeemed by Christ. They are not destroyed. Christ triumphs over them and establishes that he, as ruler over creation, is sovereign over all. Ephesians tells us that this power at work in Christ is used by God "to raise him from the dead and to make him sit at his right hand, in heaven, far above every Sovereignty, Authority, Power, or Domination, or any other name that can be named, not only in this age but also in the age to come. He has put all things under his feet, and made him, as the ruler of everything, the head of the Church; which is his body, the fullness of him who fills the whole creation" (Ephesians 1:20–23, New Jerusalem Bible).

Humanity's desire to rule its own life apart from God makes these powers and structures into idols. They, in turn, enslave humanity in their grasp. Norman Young describes concretely what happens to these powers:

They become distorted, perverted, demonic. What was good as a servant becomes evil as a master. Government, for instance, becomes tyrannical; patriotism turns into fascism; faith becomes fanaticism; mission becomes spiritual colonialism; communication turns into propaganda, education into indoctrination, technological achievement into ecological disaster.[10]

But God's work of redemption, reconciling the relationship between humanity and creation through Christ's lordship, offers the prospect of restoring the powers to their intended place of submission and service. The enslavement of these powers was broken in Christ's life, including his faithfulness unto death on the cross. In a little-noticed book, the words of Norman Young explaining Christ's confrontation with the powers on the cross, deserve our attention:

This was Jesus Christ facing the powers, refusing to give them dominion over him. Here the new age was inaugurated because one had lived out his life completely under the authority of God's kingdom while within the kingdoms of this world. The evil hold of the worldly powers was broken because Jesus had faced them and not succumbed. He had not escaped, but neither had he given them final authority by using their methods, accepting their inducements or following their ways of judging right and wrong. By refusing the rewards they offered, and refusing to fight them on their own terms even when facing their ultimate sanction of death Jesus rendered them powerless over him and put them back in their rightful place. The cross was therefore already accomplishment, not for its own sake as some kind of ritual propitiation but because the climax of obedience to the Father and unremitting love for humankind. With the resurrection came God's vindication of *this* life as victory despite apparent defeat, the life of new creation.[11]

We can add that the resurrection not only vindicated Christ's life, but demonstrated the power of God to begin the new creation. For the early church, the bodily resurrection was the proof not only that death was overcome, but that "he has put all things in subjection under his feet" (1 Corinthians 15:27). This is how Paul defended the centrality of Christ's bodily resurrection to the church at Corinth. What began with the resurrection will be culminated when "God will be all in all" (1 Corinthians 15:28).

Therefore, the bodily resurrection of Christ is the down-payment on God's pledge to win back all the creation. It is a "first fruit" of this new harvest of life. And it has already happened.

The outpouring of the Spirit, the acts of healing, the gift of tongues, the unity of the body, the eruption of a common life, the boldness of preaching, the bonds of fellowship, the joy of worship, the celebration of the Eucharist, the power for mission, and the witness to the powers were all signs for the church in Acts that the new creation had begun. And so should it be in the life of our churches today.

Like its Lord, the church is to begin living now in response to the new creation. In its evangelism, mission, and witness, it is to reclaim the word as God's creation. The promise of shalom, intended from the beginning of creation, has been inaugurated by the Prince of Peace. The ministry of the Body of Christ encompasses no less than the wholeness of humanity and all creation.

Of course your church and mine will be limited, frustrated, and imperfect in their attempts to live and serve as Christ's body in the world. Powers will seduce us. Divisions will plague us. Unfaithfulness will discourage us. Yet, ours is not the task of establishing God's new creation. Self-righteousness and vainglory would quickly defeat us in any event. Rather, we are to live by grace in response to the new creation established by Jesus Christ.

Our failures need not defeat us, for the victory is not ours, but Christ's. And his Spirit, the power of Christ's resurrection, can always freshly invade our life together.

Finally, the Spirit can never be the church's private possession. It continues to blow like the wind. We do not always know where, or when. Yet, it goes before us, and hovers again over all the world, separating light from darkness, breathing fresh life into the world, renewing the face of the earth, and bringing forth God's new creation.

As Gerard Manley Hopkins expressed in his poem "God's Grandeur":

> And though the last lights off the black West went
> Oh, morning, at the brown brink eastward, springs
> Because the Holy Ghost over the bent
> World broods with warm breast and with ah! bright wings.[12]

NOTES

1. Dennis and Rita Bennett, *The Holy Spirit and You* (Plainfield, N.J.: Logos International, 1971).

2. W. Graham Pulkingham, *Gathered for Power* (New York: Morehouse-Barlow, 1972).

3. W. Graham Pulkingham, *They Left Their Nets* (New York: Morehouse-Barlow, 1973). Another widely read book telling the story of Church of the Redeemer is Michael Harper's *A New Way of Living* (Plainfield, N.J.: Logos International, 1973). The Church of the Redeemer has gone through many changes since its renewal in the 1960s. Pulkingham was eventually sent out to minister to new Christian communities, and was based for several years at a Christian community in Scotland.

4. Leon Taylor, "New Jerusalem: Cincinnati's Charismatic Community," *Cincinnati* Magazine, February 1978, p. 49.

5. John Howard Yoder, *The Politics of Jesus* (Grand Rapids, Mich.: Eerdmans, 1972), p. 157.

6. Ibid., p. 154.

7. Ibid., p. 157.

8. Ibid., p. 158. Yoder's *Politics of Jesus* is also criticized for not spelling out concretely how the church might make contributions to the structures of society. This, however, was clearly not the intention of the book. We may hope, however, that he will address this question directly in future writings. Meanwhile, Yoder's *The Christian Witness to the State* (Newton, Kans.: Faith and Life Press, 1964) remains a classic study on the historical options of the church in relationship to political power. The short discussion of "middle axioms" and the outline of his own position (pp. 71–73) is very stimulating. Hopefully, he will elaborate on this at length.

9. Alexander Schmemann, *For the Life of the World* (St. Valdimir's Seminary Press, 1973), p. 68.

10. Norman Young, *Creator, Creation and Faith* (Philadelphia: Westminster Press, 1976). Young draws at this point on the work of Dutch theologian Albert van den Heuvel and his book *These Rebellious Powers* (London: SCM Press, 1966). The other classic, illuminating study on the subject is H. Berkhof, *Christ and the Powers* (Scottdale, Pa.: Herald Press, 1962). Yoder refers extensively to Berkhof in *Politics of Jesus*. To the examples in this quote incidentally, we must surely add militarism and economic imperialism as contemporary expressions of the powers' perversion.

11. Ibid., p. 185.

12. W. H. Gardner and N. H. Mackenzie, eds., *The Poems of Gerard Manley Hopkins* (London: Oxford University Press, 1967), p. 66.

10. The Church's Ecological Economy

During the height of the energy shortage caused by the oil embargo of the early seventies a Trappist monk said to me, "The solution to the energy crisis is love." His comment seemed irrelevant. Alternative energy technologies, renewable energy sources, changes in building codes, and more efficient transportation systems were more likely steps to actually solving the problem.

A few years later, I was listening to a Christian college faculty member give a talk about churches and energy stewardship. He included examples of several house churches and communal fellowships. Suddenly I was struck by an insight: the growth of love within church communities was the force changing people's way of life and at the same time reducing their energy consumption. My Trappist friend had a point.

When churches become concerned about ecological dangers, which is not often, those problems are usually seen as another issue to be addressed, like racism, militarism, sexism, and so on down the list. But a more accurate understanding of ecology reveals this framework to be shallow and seriously flawed.

The word ecology comes from the Greek word for house, "oikos." The same word provides the root for economy, which means, from the Greek, the management of a household's life. Ecology refers to study or understanding (from "logos") of a household's life. The word ecumenical connotes the worldwide household of God. An ecological perspective, then, sees the world as our household, and calls us to know the relationships within this dwelling place.

By definition, the church's ecological concern extends to an understanding of the church's *internal* relationships between its people and its goods, cars, clothes, water, food, energy, buildings, and so forth; and an understanding of how this web of life, called the church, relates to the world-household of life, or the creation.

Howard Snyder's helpful and provocative book *Liberating the Church,* points out six ways in which the Bible views the church and the world ecologically: The world is viewed in a long-range time frame; the natural world is seen as one interconnected whole; there is a focus on the significance of the land; there is an awareness of limits; the natural order is seen as subject to entropy; and all behavior has ecological consequences.[1] Snyder's insights demonstrate how ecological perspectives emerge within the Bible, and the strong New Testament analogy of the church as a body underscores this approach. Thus, ecology provides a framework for perceiving the church's life and relationship to creation, rather than merely presenting a set of external issues to be confronted.

The life of the church's household must be both studied and then ordered together. The church's ecology and its economy quickly become united. Any church, from the New Testament's point of view, is one household, rather than a collection of separate houses, families, and individuals. The economy of the church deals with the management of everything that is in this household.

The letters of the New Testament to early churches are written according to these principles. When, for instance, Paul writes the first letter to the church at Corinth (one of the earliest New Testament documents), one of the pastoral problems he addresses is the conduct of church members at the Lord's Supper. Apparently, the eucharistic meal was being celebrated during something like a church potluck dinner. People brought food to eat together. This was also a common practice of the guilds during that time in Corinth, and a means by which they helped provide food for members who were out of work.

But in the Corinthian church, people would "fall into sharply divided groups" (1 Corinthians 11:18). Rather than share their food together, "each of you is in such a hurry to eat his own, and

while one goes hungry another has too much to drink" (11.21).
Paul asks, "Are you so contemptuous of the church of God that
you shame its poorer members?" (11:22). The result of such actions was that the church could not properly celebrate the Lord's
Supper.

Paul then gives the instructions for communion that are part of
most every eucharistic liturgy (1 Corinthians 11:23–26). He adds
these words:

It follows that anyone who eats the bread or drinks the cup unworthily
will be guilty of desecrating the body and blood of the Lord. A man must
test himself before eating *his share* of bread and drinking from the cup. For
he who eats and drinks eats and drinks judgement on himself if he does
not discern the Body. That is why many of you are feeble and sick, and
a number have died (11:27–30). Therefore, my brothers, when you meet
for a meal, wait for one another (v. 33).

The church has puzzled over the application of these verses,
usually using them to encourage individual soul-searching. But the
context makes their meaning quite evident. Celebrating communion means that we all belong to one another. We are to receive
the gifts of life eucharistically. And if some are hoarding food
while others are going hungry, then the Body of Christ itself is
defiled, making the Lord's Supper a mockery. Economic division
in the Body of Christ and contempt for the poor in its midst dese-
crate the Body and Blood of the Lord.

Paul's warning is directed to anyone who partakes in the Body
of Christ without examining his or her economic separation from
other members and insensitivity to their needs, both of which
directly contradict the whole meaning of belonging to the Body of
Christ. Communion, the celebration of God's gift to the church of
life through Jesus Christ, is disgraced. As Paul wrote, a few verses
earlier, "When we break bread, is it not a means of sharing in the
Body of Christ? Because there is one loaf, we, many as we are, are
one body; for it is one loaf of which we all partake" (1 Corinthians
10:16–17).

Because these truths were not being followed, the whole Body was suffering. Perhaps some members were sick and feeble because they literally did not have enough nourishment. But also, these divisions obviously squelched the restoring, healing work of God's Spirit.

Paul immediately follows his pastoral discourse on communion with his teaching on gifts and the church as Christ's Body, in 1 Corinthians 12. "For Christ is like a single body with its many limbs and organs, which, many as they are, together make up one body" (12:12). "God has combined the various parts of the body, giving special honour to the humbler parts, so that there might be no sense of division in the body, but that all its organs might feel the same concern for one another" (vv. 24–25).

There could hardly be a more powerful way to describe ecologically how everything in the church belongs to one whole. Further, Paul follows these insights with an admonition to seek the higher gifts, especially the gift of love (1 Corinthians 13). For without the outpouring of this gift, there can be no life for the Body of Christ. In concrete, practical, daily expressions, love fortifies the life of the Body of Christ. This love, the gift of the Spirit, orders the household of faith; it manages all those things that are a part of the body; it is the guiding feature of the church's economy.

Possessing money simply means having the power to obtain objects or services. For the churches in the New Testament, this power was to be shared together, and money given on the basis of need. Certainly, this was the model assumed by Paul, and one that was governed by love and based on the belonging of all to one body.

Paul did not hesitate to apply this model among churches as well as within them. The Body of Christ was to display an ecumenical economy. For if the worldwide household of the church was in fact just that—an ecumenical body—then the management of its life, including the money of its members, should be shared together in order to meet the needs of the whole household.

Spiritual unity must have practical consequences. Perhaps no struggle vexed Paul as deeply as the conflict between Jewish and Gentile Christians in the church. Galatians was written in direct response to this pastoral issue, and Paul struggled with the theology of these questions toward the end of the Book of Romans, particularly in Chapters 9–11.[2]

Paul's insistence that there is no distinction between Jew and Greek (Galatians 3:28, Romans 10:12) had a practical effect in response to serious financial need within the church at Jerusalem. The causes of that need are not entirely clear. It may have resulted in part because the huge influx of Jewish converts after Pentecost became "victims of social and economic ostracism, ecclesiastical excommunication, and national disinheritance. Their business enterprises must in most cases have collapsed in ruins and family bonds been heartbreakingly severed."[3]

While the common sharing described in Acts responded in part to these conditions, the needs continued to be overwhelming. And "the care for the poor was an essential task which the church had to perform."[4] On Paul's visits to Jerusalem, he witnessed the poverty there. On his second visit he brought contributions from Christians in Antioch "for the relief of fellow-Christians in Judea" (Acts 11:29). And at the Council of Jerusalem five years later, Peter, James, and John asked that Paul and Barnabas continue to remember the poor at Jerusalem while doing their work among the Gentiles, which, Paul tells the Galatians, he was zealous to do (Galatians 2:10).

Paul was constantly concerned for the financially impoverished Christians in Jerusalem. More than merely a response to their need, this was for Paul a practical test of a church's commitment to truly being part of the Body of Christ. One preoccupation of his pastoral work was to build this unity through the financial sharing of Gentile Christians with the Jerusalem Church. Both letters to the church at Corinth bring up the subject—the entire eighth and ninth chapters of 2 Corinthians are devoted to this topic.

To the Corinthians, Paul stressed that this giving was a response to grace. Not only does it meet those in need, it expresses thanksgiving to God (2 Corinthians 9:12). Because they have received such lavish grace, their response to the needs of Christ's Body should be marked by an equally lavish outpouring of their gifts to its need. He appeals directly to Christ's example: "For you know how generous our Lord Jesus Christ has been; he was rich, yet for your sake he became poor, so that through his poverty you might become rich" (8:9).

A generous response by the people to this great need in the church, even across what were then vast geographical and cultural barriers, could demonstrate the reality of the church's love and be a confession of the gospel (2 Corinthians 9:13). "It is a question of equality. At the moment your surplus meets their need, but one day your need may be met from their surplus. The aim is equality; as the Scripture has it, 'The man who got much had no more than enough, and the man who got little did not go short' " (8:14–15). The quotation comes from Exodus, describing the manna that fell each day to be gathered by the children of Israel in the wilderness. When gathered, it was distributed so each person would have as much as he or she could eat. None could be hoarded, for it molded and became bug-infested by the next day. Greed was condemned and mutuality was encouraged, all in response to the provision of daily bread through God's grace. The manna was God's gift, and so was the money of those in the church at Corinth.

For the early church as for the church today the meaning is clear: we as people do not just belong to one another; rather, in our relationship to the creation we belong to one another in the Body of Christ. Remembering the root meanings of the words, we can say that Paul describes the ecology of the ecumenical church, and suggests an economic response.

The specific methods of the church's economy in the New Testament were not uniform. The common pooling of all resources within the Jerusalem church described in Acts 2 and 4 was the concrete response, prompted by the Spirit's power, to their need within that social setting. And that method has continued to be empowering and liberating for various faith communities throughout the history of the church.

That method, however, was probably not typical of the early churches. Clearly, it was not the case at Corinth. Paul's instructions for their collection of gifts for Jerusalem makes this evident: "Each of you is to put aside and keep by him a sum in proportion to his gains" (1 Corinthians 16:2). And while the content of the letters to the Corinthians, pastorally responding to countless problems, would restrain us from holding up any area of its life as a model, still Paul never urges them, or any other church, to adopt the internal economic method of the Jerusalem community.

The "equality" spoken of by Paul between the Jerusalem church and the churches at Corinth and elsewhere could not have meant a rigidly equal distribution of money amongst them—obviously this would have been an impossibility. However, it was a powerful declaration of economic reciprocity and mutuality—as essential to a church's life as a nervous system is to a body. Surplus meets need.

The specific administration of a church's economy in the New Testament seems to have been determined by its practical circumstances. But the guiding principles and purposes were not the least bit voluntary. Rather, the church's economy was seen as a direct expression of membership in the Body of Christ, and a sign of its unity.

These New Testament guidelines are clear:

Everything the Body of Christ has belongs to God. Like the manna in the wilderness and the Body and Blood of the Eucharist, members of the church only gather and partake of what are God's gifts. The New Testament letters never appeal to the Old Testament tithe as a method. Its vision was more abandoned, avoiding any notion that 10 percent belonged to God, and the rest to the people.[5]

Members of the church share economically with one another. Being in Christ means living in the household of faith. In that household, we belong to one another. Severing our economic lives from the body results in a spiritual separation as well.

Sharing is a response to need. The economic methods of the church mentioned in the New Testament—the pooling of resources at Jerusalem, the appointing of deacons, and the collections for the Jerusalem church—all were particular ways of meeting pressing needs. And they were concrete ways of making the Body's spiritual unity a physical reality.

The church's economy—how it manages its household—must flow from its ecology, or its understanding of its relationships within itself and with creation. This is the testimony of the New Testament. In the church's first centuries its stance toward money and possessions continued to be molded by this witness. In the fourth century, St. John Chrysostom, for instance, wrote:

> Mark the wise dispensation of God: That he might put mankind to shame, he has made certain things common, as the sun, air, earth, and water, whose benefits are dispensed equally to all as brethren. . . . Observe, that concerning things that are common there is no contention, but all is peaceable. But when one attempts to possess himself of anything, to make it his own, then contention is introduced, as if nature herself were indignant, that when God brings us together in every way, we are eager to divide and separate ourselves by appropriating things, and by using those cold words "mine and thine." Then there is contention and uneasiness. But where this is not, no strife or contention is bred. This state therefore is rather our inheritance, and more agreeable to nature.[6]

By now, you might agree with these perspectives in general. But like me, you're wondering what to do about your Toyota Tercel.

The distance between the New Testament's view of the church's economy and that of the average American congregation today seems staggering. The personal questions and issues we often begin with seem disjointed from the biblical vision. Can I eat at McDonald's? Often? Should I buy a new sports coat? Should I raise alfalfa sprouts? Likewise, for our local church. Can we make our budget? Shall we build a new educational wing? How do we solve our parking problem?

Today's typical church members grant far more authority over their economic lives to the federal government than to their own congregation. Without reluctance, we share with the Internal Revneue Service a detailed description of how money has flowed in and out of our lives over a year. Further, we pay a percentage of that money to support the government in proportion to what we have earned. We have virtually no say as to how that money is spent, and we are usually willing to have this money taken directly from our pay checks, so that we never see it.

In speaking to the congregations of various churches, I have proposed at times that those in small fellowship groups simply share their tax returns with one another. Often, the response is an embarrassed silence. Yet, why should we hesitate at telling those whom we belong to as Christ's Body what we have already confessed to the government?

Within most churches, members still hold to the fiction that their economic lives are private and can be separated from their spiritual fellowship. In so doing, the plain witness of the New Testament is dismissed. Even in pastoral settings, parishioners are more apt to confess sexual temptation and sin than to confide about the lust for money. How often do we seek pastoral counsel about buying a new car?

Most of us need to start not by learning to like lentils, but by being open about the economic facts of our lives with one another. Our enslavement to the power of money will not be broken as long as we protect our economic privacy. Secret areas of our lives are always fertile ground for sin. Confession, sharing, and trust are the pathways for God's redemptive power to work in our lives.

We need not be anxious about whether our economic lives are righteous. They are not. We can begin, however, by making our personal economics transparent. This first step we can take because we believe that we belong to one Body. Our true household is the church. The way we can put our own household in order is to join it to the economy of the church. Again, economy reflects ecology. How can we, then, cling to a private economy while claiming we belong to the church? And beyond that, how can we say we belong to God?

What is at stake is not just our money, or our personal budget, but our relationship to God's creation. Money is just the primary means for exercising that relationship. That is why, in and of itself, it is not evil. After all, we all are part of the creation. Money is "the root of all evil" simply because it is the means by which we can distort our relationship to creation, including one another.

Becoming economically transparent to others often requires becoming more open with ourselves. How do we actually regard the clothes we wear and the food we eat? And how do those things affect the creation? What about our place of shelter, where we live? Our means of travel? Our sources of entertainment and recreation? What role is money playing in relationship to these dimensions of life? And in what or in whom do we trust to see that these are provided?

One tool that may be helpful in answering these questions is writing a "money autobiography."[7] Explaining its purpose one person wrote: "As we discern the ways we earn, inherit, invest, spend, give or waste money—often without conscious choice or a deliberate faith stance—we will be enabled to more fully respond to Jesus. . . . The Spirit cannot free us to be communities of liberation if we are in bondage to an ancient idol."[8] A short excerpt from another such reflection went like this:

I am aware as I write this that there is a great deal of avoidance in my dealing with money. I am also aware that I fall prey to the trap of simplifying my life with the best woodstove on the market, if I can borrow enough money to buy it. As I continue to wrestle with this in myself, with God's help, I have to admit that I am about far enough along to identify some of the demons, but only beginning to confront them.[9]

Sharing such insights within our faith communities is surely as important as being open about our tax returns. These are practical ways to help make all our lives more accessible to God and one another, and to make creation more accessible to us as God's gift.

Such sharing leads to a mutuality in the economic decisions we make. We are relieved from attempting to govern our economic lives in isolation. For most of us that is a losing battle anyway, given the unremitting pressures of modern consumer society to make those choices for us. Freedom from the powers means, concretely, that through the Body of Christ, economic life for its members can be reclaimed by God. And without this, how can the church be a vessel for pointing to God's new creation?

The methods for organizing the church's economy will differ in our time, just as in the New Testament. But for us, as for them, the structures we choose should arise in response to need, rather than as some charter designed to give us an institutional purity or security.

For many congregations, responding to need is difficult, for the economically needy are not in their midst. Furthermore, our relationship to those needs can be buffered in a variety of ways. The deacons take care of special cases. The home mission board is serving the inner-city poor. The relief agency is reaching the hungry. For some individuals and congregations, giving money serves to keep the needy at arms length.

The easiest remedy to this danger is to relocate the church in an area of need. Several emerging church communities have done just that. As a body of people, they move to a place of economic need. Of course, many more congregations, responding to urban changes, have done just the opposite.

Short of relocation, the other possibility is to form intentional relationships with the poor. Church-to-church contacts, stretching across economic and cultural divisions, can facilitate this. Likewise, specific mission projects can do the same. While doing research for several weeks away from home on this book, I visited one affluent church in the Midwest at the time its congregation decided its members would spend at least a week of their summer vacation working at a church camp that reached out to the poor and disadvantaged in the Appalachian mountains.

For them and for others, such relationships can be a way to encounter need, both within other parts of Christ's Body and within the world. The vitality of these relationships can then shape the economic choices we make and help mold the structures adopted for our church's economy.

Human needs are not the only needs to which we must respond. Reclaiming the world as God's means the church is drawn to the suffering of the whole creation. The church must get to know the earth's wounds from strip-mining, the water's decay from spilled chemicals, the land's agony from eroded soil, the rainforest's injury from clear cutting, and the lake's death from acid rain. Though our lives are intertwined with creation, we can blind ourselves to its oppression as easily as we can protect ourselves from the poor. Yet, connections to the suffering of both often can be made within our own household.

Only when we entrust our lives to God can we open our economic lives to the church and relate to the needs of creation. Creation then breaks forth to us as new.

One of the fruits of spiritual transformation is a new simplicity within the Body of Christ and in the style of our life. We learn that we live by grace—not just spiritually, but physically. Again, the two cannot be separated, for they are part of the whole. The God who creates is the God who redeems.

Recent years have produced a number of fine books on "simple lifestyles."[10] Practical advice about how to live simply is readily available. Little need be added here; furthermore, my personal way of life is still far from benefitting from the worthy proposals I have read and agreed with. But based on our biblical exploration of creation and redemption, we can make certain observations, and many of these have been borne out by my personal experience.

Lifestyle must always be rooted in grace. The way we live is to be a response to God's grace, which has flowed to us and to all creation in Jesus Christ. Through this grace, all of life is tranformed and becomes eucharistic.

At times, we are prone to try to simplify our lives because so much of material life in our society simply seems bad. And it is—bad for us and even worse for the world. Yet, in this attempt we miss the point of the gospel. A simplified lifestyle should grow out of the realization that creation is good and a precious gift of grace to be cherished.

Because we see creation as God's provision for all people, we treat it as such, in celebration. This is what changes our lifestyle. The forms this takes are countless. We buy organic food because we treasure God's earth. We boycott name-brand pineapples because their fields in the Philippines should belong not to a multinational corporation but to the people. We buy second-hand clothes in order to free resources in response to need. We compost our garbage and recycle cans because those things are not disposable, but useful. Even these small steps are responses to Christ's work of redemption.

But even these brief examples raise an obvious problem. Isn't it impossible to formulate a "pure" lifestyle? Won't there always be ways in which what we eat, or drink, or wear, or where we live, or how we travel will contribute to someone else's oppression or cause some defilement of the creation? For us who live within modern consumer society, the answer is yes.

A totally guilt-free lifestyle cannot be found. Trying to do so would eventually spawn such casuistry that it would bewilder the best Jesuit. That is why guilt can never truly be a motive for changing lifestyles. It can never be fully dispelled. Furthermore, to the extent such attempts seem to succeed, they often produce self-righteousness.

Even though guilt is always with us and should be with us when we consider the consequences of our actions, grace must mold and prompt the changes we make. And those changes, as we have said, will best be nurtured corporately, as an expression of our life and unity in Christ's Body. God's grace will fill Christ's Body, flowing out to creation and returning in thanksgiving to God. Paul appealed pastorally to the Corinthian church on the basis of this grace, telling them that God "who provides seed for the sowing and bread for food will provide the seed for you to sow; he will multiply it and swell the harvest of your benevolence, and you will always be rich enough to be generous. Through our action such generosity will issue in thanksgiving to God, . . . their hearts will go out to you because of the richness of the grace which God has imparted to you" (2 Corinthians 9:10–12, 14).

We can never, of course, do enough. But the power of grace comes not from setting standards of perfection, but by liberating us through love in ever deepening ways. We act not because we're guilty, but because we're thankful.

Such mutuality and sharing within the global household, simply implementing the precepts commended by the New Testament, would have revolutionary effects in our own time. Without any hesitation, Paul organized a redistribution of wealth within the early Christian community, seeing this as a compelling pastoral question and devoting considerable time and energy to its implementation in the course of his ministry. Such a redistribution, as we have seen, crossed geographical, cultural, and economic barriers that must have seemed just as formidable in that time as any do today. If the Lord of the Church is truly the prince of global shalom, the biblical call for sharing surplus to meet need could hardly be more urgent in our time of such astonishing divisions of global resources.

The emphasis of the New Testament letters is on sharing among the sectors of the church, though not limited to that arena. For instance, "As opportunity offers, let us work for the good of all, especially members of the household of faith" (Galatians 6:10). The indisputable thrust of biblical theology concerning the oppressed and poor, however, directs us to a vision of global justice for all; even more, to shalom for the whole creation. Yet, if the church is to seek this end in its mission, then it must reflect the overcoming of such divisions in its own life. Thus, building an ecumenical economy within the church may be the proper way to begin, and that can start even between a congregation in Des Moines, Iowa, and one in Port au Prince, Haiti.

The potential of acting out such an ecumenical economy is enormous. In 1977, Ron Sider estimated that if the average nuclear family in a church accepted a standard of living only about 30 percent lower than the median for U.S. families and gave their surplus income to meet pressing global needs, the entire 5 billion dollars requested by developing countries at the 1974 World Food Conference for agricultural assistance could be met from just 10 million Christians.[11] Richard Taylor, writing a stewardship guide for the American Lutheran Church, estimated that a similar response by Lutherans could increase the budget of Lutheran World Relief by one thousand percent, to 4.5 billion dollars.[12]

The fact is that the wealth of church members in affluent countries, if distributed as suggested by biblical teaching and example, could restructure the global economy. The early church used the word "oikoumene" to describe the world as one, or as 'the whole inhabited earth in God."[13] If the church were to accept its true ecological setting in the world, it would begin building an ecumenical economy rooted in God's grace through Jesus Christ.

We have spoken of the church's economy as all that belongs to the members of the Body of Christ. For many, however, practical questions remain on the agenda, like the need for a new parking lot. Perhaps they aren't the right questions, but they still need a response. So we turn our attention to the bricks and mortar of the actual buildings we call churches.[14]

About 90 billion dollars worth of real estate is used for religious purposes in the United States. New church buildings have been going up at a cost of 1 billion dollars a year.[15] Denominations have whole divisions devoted to assisting the financing of new church buildings. But in light of the church's global commitment, we must ask whether we really need all these buildings, and whether they help or hinder an ecumenical economy. It is heartening to know that the early church, with its rapid growth and fervent life, made it through almost three centuries before building sanctuaries for worship. House churches—an ancient church tradition—might be more compatible to our membership in the global household of faith.

Yet, what about the church buildings that will endure, and the new ones that will be built? First, structures erected by the church should express a redeemed relationship to creation. They should cooperate with the earth, and treat its resources as shared gifts.

Church architecture has long sought to express a people's relationship to God and to each other. But rarely has it tried to express the relationship between God, humanity, and the creation except perhaps in negative ways. Some church structures strive to lift the congregation out of earth toward heaven.

For example, a church near a home where I lived for a short

time in Michigan is designed with a roof that looks much like a ski jump. The building is rectangular in shape, and from the top of the ski jump, down to the ground, the whole wall across the width of the building is glass. Inside, a cross is suspended, and the congregation faces the glass wall.

The intention is worthy. The church reaches up and out toward God. But there is one serious flaw. The building faces due north. The solid glass wall is actually sheltered from the sun and faces the cold north wind. I can only guess what rising energy prices did to the church's budget. Its zeal to be heavenly minded obscured any sense of its orientation to the earth. If the same building had been turned to the south, it might have made a more suitable statement about the creation.

A study in 1980 estimated that there were no more than twenty churches in the United States designed to utilize solar energy.[16] If we are to have buildings in which to worship, then let them speak of the new creation brought about by Christ. Let them be structures that cherish the gifts of creation. Let the earth not be their foe, but their shelter. Let God's light of creation provide their heat. And let the wind that blows like the Spirit keep them cool and refreshed. Let those structures be a witness by their very design to Christ's redeeming love for the world.

These are all readily available technological options. Moreover, they can deepen theological awareness. A quote from a study examining the handful of solar-powered churches underscores the sensitivity of these congregations to earthkeeping:

They were aware of the stewardship that humankind should exhibit toward the divinely given resources of the earth and the heavens. We cannot say whether this awareness grew out of their involvement in building solar churches, or whether they decided to build solar churches because they were so aware. Probably both.[17]

When the new St. Paul's Center Church in Springfield, Oregon, had grown to one hundred fifty people in 1978, the congregation decided to build a sanctuary based on alternative energy and utilize volunteer labor. The structure is partially earth bermed, with a southward-facing passive solar glass wall and large solar collectors.

The congregation wrote an "energy covenant," which members and others were invited to sign:

In the Christian context the community basis for the movement toward responsible stewardship of energy is called the "church." The worshipping, working community of faith is a natural entity for cooperating in understanding, acting, and being accountable for our good earth's resources. We will:

1. Advocate energy conservation measures locally, in our state and federal governments
2. Promote development of alternative, renewable energy resources
3. Publicize alternatives in energy conservation, from the cost effectiveness of solar energy to cooperative gardening
4. Encourage carpooling
5. Monitor our church's solar heating facility to determine its impact on other churches and similar structures, and publish the findings, making the information available to all interested[18]

The average existing church building is often economically restrained from being retrofitted with solar technology. But there are exceptions. In Washingtonville, New York, the First Presbyterian Church built a do-it-yourself solar collector using several recycled materials and volunteer labor. The cost was $540, paid for by their men's council. In 1978, they saved $500 on their oil bills.[19] Any church structure can make substantial improvements by conserving energy. The State of Massachusetts prepared a publication titled *Reducing Energy Costs in Religious Buildings.*[20] It outlines simple, economical steps that will immediately save 20 percent of a church building's energy costs.

Besides church buildings, consider all the camps, ranches, and retreat centers operated by denominations and para-church groups. They are a vast potential resource for on-site theological education in care for the earth. More than offering a brief respite in the midst of nature, these facilities could teach people how to care for the creation.

Holden Village at Lake Chelan, Washington, is a well-known Lutheran conference site, filled through the summer with families who come for courses on various theological themes, Bible study, and recreation. The village is a self-contained community reached only by boat. And with over three hundred people regularly present, it must provide its own energy supply, waste disposal, and other functions necessary to a small town.

Water from a mountain stream runs a mini-hydro generator supplying electricity. Solar collectors heat the hot water for the laundry. A new building, used throughout the year, is heated by passive solar design and wood stoves. At meals in the dining hall, leftovers on plates are separated by each person into "compostables"—food wastes which will compost—and "combustibles" such as napkins, bones, and other things. The first are emptied after each meal into well-designed compost bins. Combined with other organic wastes, rich compost for soil is created in two to three weeks. The burnable material is used with wood for various energy needs.

The compost, in one experiment, has been dumped on unfertile ground that has been contaminated by tailings from the abandoned copper mine that caused the village to be built originally. Vegetables are now grown there from the compost—demonstrating a successful attempt to reclaim that piece of earth and heal its wounds. When last I visited, plans called for Jerusalem artichokes to be grown there. Methane from their wastes would meet the fuel needs of the village's few motorized vehicles. Wood is cut on a small-scale sawmill, an example of creative appropriate technology, and dried in a solar kiln. Even the sauna is wood-heated.

Moreover, the village is run by volunteers—often college students—who come at their own expense to experience the joy and fellowship of this place. Even the faculty members who do the teaching, including some of the church's leading theologians, come at their own expense and on the condition that they will volunteer to work in the kitchen.

The whole place tries to run on grace—God's grace in the creation and the grace of volunteers, and in this way guests who come pay only modest fees. Holden is but one example, full of flaws like anywhere else, but a living example of what is possible in such settings once we affirm that the earth is the Lord's.

The previously mentioned study group that visited solar churches made this unanticipated discovery:

Whether or not there is a direct correlation in congregations between warmth that comes from the sun and warmth demonstrated by members toward each other and to strangers is unproven. But the experience of the Solar Building Working Group in the on-site visits seems to indicate that a sensitivity to sun power is accompanied by a warm, outgoing sense of caring for people.[21]

The Trappist monk who claimed that love could resolve the energy crisis showed rare discernment.

NOTES

1. Howard Snyder, *Liberating the Church* (Downers Grove, Ill.: InterVarsity Press, 1983), pp. 45–50.
2. A few commentators have argued that this, in fact, is the whole focus of Romans. Krister Stendahl has advanced this perspective. Despite my admiration for much of Stendahl's work (my son is even named Jon Krister), I am unpersuaded by his argument on this point.
3. Philip E. Hughes, *The Second Epistle to the Corinthians,* (Grand Rapids: Eerdmans, 1962), p. 284. This book is part of *The New International Commentary on the New Testament.*
4. F. W. Grosheide, *The First Epistle to the Corinthians* (Grand Rapids; Eerdmans, 1953), p. 397. This is also part of *The New International Commentary.*
5. See, for example, Richard Foster, *Freedom of Simplicity* (San Francisco: Harper & Row, 1981), pp. 24, 49–50. I would not argue against a tithe ever being used as a method, but only point out that tithing is more modest a practice in both spirit and style than what existed in the early church and is commended in the New Testament.
6. Jim Halteman, "The Economics of the Believers' Church," unpublished manuscript, p. 10.
7. Elizabeth O'Conner, *Letters to Scattered Pilgrims* (San Francisco: Harper & Row, 1979), pp. 28–30.
8. From a pamphlet by Catherine Snow, *Writing a Money Autobiography,* p. 2, available from the Ministry of Money, 11301 Neelsville Church Rd., Germantown, MD 20874. This group, headed by Dan McClanen, is a ministry affiliated with Church of the Saviour in Washington, D.C., Elizabeth O'Conner's home church.
9. Ibid., p. 4.

10. Richard Foster, *Freedom of Simplicity,* and his earlier *Celebration of Discipline* (San Francisco: Harper & Row, 1978) integrate spirituality and simplicity well. A few other examples are John Taylor, *Enough Is Enough* (London: SCM Press, 1975); Ron Sider, *Rich Christians in an Age of Hunger* (Downers Grove, Ill.: Intervarsity Press, 1977); Doris Janzen Longacre, *Living More with Less* (Scottdale, Pa.: Herald Press, 1980). Together, these combine theology, biblical study, spirituality, economic analysis, and practical suggestions. Many others, of course, could be added.

11. Ron Sider, "Sharing the Wealth: the Church as Biblical Model for Public Policy," *Christian Century,* June 8, 1977, p. 564. Sider's article is quoted in the study guide cited in the next footnote.

12. Richard K. Taylor, *A Community of Stewards: A Congregational Guide to the Stewardship of Consumption* (Minneapolis: Augsburg Publishing House, 1978), p. 9.

13. Larry Rasmussen, *Economic Anxiety and Christian Faith* (Minneapolis: Augsburg Publishing House, 1981), p. 61.

14. Our habit of calling buildings where we worship "churches" is confusing and theologically misleading. The word is derived from words meaning "the Lord's house." Only some pagans would believe that God lived in a building. I once saw a sign on a church building which read something like "The Rosemont Church of Christ meets here." That, at least, was clarifying.

15. Richard K. Taylor, *Community of Stewards,* p. 14.

16. "Solar Churches," *Grapevine* 12, no. 4 (October 1980): 6. *Grapevine* is the publication of the Joint Strategy and Action Committee, 475 Riverside Dr., New York, NY, headed by John DeBoer.

17. Ibid., p. 6.

18. Ibid., p. 6. A recent book, *The Solar Church,* by Jennifer A. Adams (New York: The Pilgraim Press, 1982) documents further the existence of solar-designed churches.

19. Ibid., p. 7.

20. *Reducing Energy Costs in Religious Buildings,* produced by the Massachusetts Energy Office, Boston, 1978.

21. "Solar Churches," p. 7.

11. Global Sanctification

For the third year in a row in south India, the monsoon was weak and failing. The reservoirs were alarmingly low. Driving across the state of Tamil Nadu, my Indian friend pointed to patches of dry land with standing water. "There used to be trees there. But some years ago, the government had them cut. Now nothing holds the water. We lose so much from evaporation."

Was reforestation being attempted? I asked. "Yes, there are some examples. But this becomes difficult because villagers take the wood for cooking."

The K. V. Kuppam Block in that region (a block is similar to a township) includes one hundred thousand people. Seventy-five percent live at a standard below the poverty line as set by the Indian government—on an income of ninty-five dollars per year. One out of four children between one and four die, usually from diarrhea or dysentery. In 1977, the Rural Unit for Health and Social Affairs (RUHSA) was begun there by the nearby Vellore Christian Medical Hospital and College. Long reknowned as a leading medical institution in India, Vellore had begun focusing more attention on the basic needs of the rural poor. And in six years, RUHSA had become a highly praised model of integrated rural development in India.

But its Director, Daleep Mukarji, was also worried in 1983 about the weak monsoon. He showed me a model project in which jasmine plants were grown by using drip irrigation. RUH-SA was trying to introduce various agricultural methods for conserving water. I asked him about the level of the water table. "Officials have said that it is not going down very much. But our own measurements show a sharp decline," he answered.

This area of India was part of the Green Revolution. Electricity spread through the region, enabling electric pumps to pull water up for widespread irrigation. A decade ago, experts in international aid applauded the progress. But like America's Great Plains, the ground water in Tamil Nadu is being pumped out far faster than the rains are replacing it.

Back in the United States, a denomination's director of World Mission confessed his uneasiness over a south Indian church group's funding request on his desk. "They just want to dig the well deeper," he lamented. "Of course you want to help them, for the situation is serious. But this is no long-term solution."

A letter I received later from Daleep Mukarji underlined the same point:

As we go through the third year of the drought, we are conscious that it is not only the shortfall in the monsoons, but the fact that our underground water resources have been overexploited that makes this drought so serious. Obviously, weaker sections suffer most, as they are unable to get jobs, with little or no agricultural production. And they have often to travel three to four kilometers to get water.

Mukarji was saying that economy depended on ecology. The life of the one hundred thousand people in the K. V. Kuppam Block, like anywhere else, depended on the creation. Only there, it was more obvious. The massive technology that blurs these connections for those who live in affluent societies is not present. The shortage of water reserves stifling agricultural production would effect the poor first and most sharply.

For Mukarji, this raised the need for what he called "development theology," a theology that would help us to recognize the patterns of exploitation not only between people, but toward the creation. His letter continued:

We have got to have a theological basis for an understanding of God's creation and the stewardship role that we have over His resources. In this context, we must live more simply and more sensibly so others can simply live. This is very much in keeping with the overall mission of healing, health, and wholeness and something in which we, as individuals, professional people, and Christians, need to get involved in.

Grasping the ecology of the ecumenical church will dramatically alter our theology and practice of world mission. Since creation itself is the recipient of God's salvation, the church's missionary activity must not take place simply in the whole earth; it must include the whole earth. The scope of Christ's redemption beckons mission work not only to soul-saving, but also to earthkeeping.

Ghillean Prance, a noted expert on the Amazon rainforest, is also a Christian deeply troubled by missionaries' lack of ecological awareness. He writes:

With the Paraguay Indians, and in similar cases I have seen first-hand in Brazil, the greatest misunderstanding is failure to recognize the paramount importance to the Indian peoples of their land, and of their communal ownership of it. To change the Indians by insisting on the importance of private property, or to turn them into cotton pickers who earn a daily wage against their wills, is a serious infringement of both their basic human rights and of the thousands of years of experience such people have had in working out an ecology appropriate for their forest region.[1]

Prance's observations underscore the dangers of mission work carried out without a redemptive sensitivity toward humanity's earthly home.

Our understanding of the church as a body can deepen our awareness of what causes creation's wounds. When one member suffers, all the parts feel the suffering. The shortage of water in India, like the examples from South America, reveal how our technology and cultural influences can become part of the problem rather than the solution. Yet, still as one body, suffering can be used for redemptive purposes. A new sense of water as God's gift might transform our agricultural relationship to the earth in both Tamil Nadu and Nebraska. Tribes in the Amazon could actually teach missionaries about the care of the earth, if they were open to such instruction. And through the ecumenical belonging to the Body of Christ, a healing could come to creation, building shalom.

These dimensions of world mission underscore the church's need to counteract the threats to creation's integrity and survival.

We can now turn our attention to the most critical of these dangers.

Nuclear crisis. The nuclear threat is an indication of humanity's destructive power over earth's creation. The church's response in the last few years to this danger has been to become alert, discerning, and increasingly committed to resistance and peacemaking. Little need be added here to the scores of perceptive articles, books, study guides, and educational resources that have appeared in the course of this awakening.[2] The call of *Sojourners* magazine for a "new abolitionist movement" against nuclear arms has fallen on fertile soil.

The biblical threads of creation and redemption, which we have seen woven through the heart of Scripture, suggest two observations to all of us in the church who are opposed to the threat and the very existence of nuclear weapons.

First, like any campaign striving for a focus, opposition to the nuclear arms race has tended to be separated from other issues. Since single-issue movements are the name of the game in the politics of modern protest, it is not surprising that the nuclear question generally has followed suit.

The church's opposition to the nuclear danger has become deeply rooted in worship, Bible study, and prayer, calling forth sacrificial protest and even growing civil disobedience. But deep roots should also produce broad branches reaching out to all the creation.

A secular author, Jonathan Schell, first drew strong attention to the links between nuclear and ecological concerns. His influential book *The Fate of the Earth* raised theological questions about humanity's relationship to the creation in light of the capacity for nuclear destruction. Schell wrote: "The nuclear peril is usually seen in isolation from the threats to other forms of life and their ecosystems, but in fact it should be seen as the very center of the ecological crisis."[3] Schell got to this insight primarily through an exhaustive study of the actual effects of a widespread nuclear exchange. This is a summary of his findings:

Bearing in mind that the possible consequences of the detonation of thousands of megatons of nuclear explosives include the blinding of insects, birds, and beasts all over the world; the extinction of many ocean species, among them some at the base of the food chain; the temporary or permanent alteration of the climate of the globe, with the outside chance of "dramatic" and "major" alterations in the structure of the atmosphere; the pollution of the whole ecosphere with oxides of nitrogen; the incapacitation in ten minutes of unprotected people who go out into the sunlight; the blinding of people who go out into the sunlight; a significant decrease in photosynthesis in plants around the world; the scalding and killing of many crops; the increase in rates of cancer and mutation around the world, but especially in the targeted zones, and the attendant risk of global epidemics; the possible poisoning of all vertebrates by sharply increased levels of Vitamin D in their skin as a result of increased ultraviolet light; and the outright slaughter on all targeted continents of most human beings and other living things by the initial nuclear radiation, the firefalls, the thermal pulses, the blast waves, the mass fires, and the fallout from the explosions; and, considering that these consequences will all interact with one another in unguessable ways and, furthermore, are in all likelihood an incomplete list, which will be added to as our knowledge of the earth increases, one must conclude that a full-scale nuclear holocaust could lead to the extinction of mankind.[4]

In this analysis of destruction, Schell sensed the obvious relatedness of creation and humanity. We have been accustomed to think of war as violence between people. But the nature of nuclear weapons drives home the truth that this is war against the earth.

Acquiring the god-like powers to destroy the creation was confessed by those who made and decided to use the first atomic bomb. Upon seeing the first test bomb successfully exploded in New Mexico, its chief inventor, J. Robert Oppenheimer, quoted a Hindu text:

> If the radiance of a thousand suns
> Were to burst at once into the sky,
> That would be like the splendor
> Of the Mighty One.
> I am become Death
> The shatterer of worlds.[5]

And President Truman, announcing that the bomb had been dropped on Hiroshima, boasted: "It is the harnessing of the basic power of the universe. . . . What we have done is the greatest achievement of organized science in history."[6]

Before all else theologically, the nuclear threat epitomizes humanity's desire to claim God's power and seize the creation. Nuclear arsenals are the technological fulfillment of the fall. This fact places the nuclear danger at the heart of humanity's relationship to the creation. The church's response, then, must flow from its understanding of creation and redemption. And that response will find natural connections to the ecology and economy of the whole world.

This second observation follows quite sensibly. The church's response should flow more from the joy of cherishing the creation than from the horror of its annihilation. Such affirmation should sound louder than the cries of resistance. Love should cast out fear.

Opposition to nuclear weapons has grown, in part, as people have become freshly aware of their terror. This has been necessary, for previously the reality of nuclear holocaust had been distant from people's consciousness. Yet the exposure to that horror, while essential, will eventually prompt either a despair or else frenzied acts of anguish, unless a ground for hope is found.

For the church this hope is in Jesus Christ, who entered into the heart of the creation, triumphed over its darkness on the cross, and won it back for God. The nuclear horror can be overcome because redemption has touched creation. In Christ we know that the world is loved. This love for the world, incarnate in our life as Christ's Body on earth, is the power that can actually seek out the abolition of nuclear weapons.

The biblical view of creation, and its declaration of God's redemptive work in Jesus Christ, reshapes our relationship to all the earth's resources, as we have seen. In its ministry of restoration, the church should serve both as a model and point to specific directions for society to take that will nurture the wholeness of creation. Here, we can simply outline some of those directions, indicating areas for further fruitful exploration.

Economic vision. Earlier we explored how both Adam Smith and Karl Marx adopted the same position toward the exploitation of nature as a premise of their economic theories. The practical consequences of this position in capitalist as well as socialist societies are easily distinguished. The onslaught of consumer forces within modern market-oriented economies promotes needs so persistently that the exploitation of nature is constantly accelerated. The commercials broadcast during just one feature-length movie on television, ABC's showing of *An Unmarried Woman,* make the point. Here is the schedule:

9:01:20	Miller Beer
9:01:50	Dove Soap
9:02:20	Close-Up Toothpaste
9:02:50	Halls Lozenges
9:03:20	FILM BEGINS
9:32:05	Breck Shampoo
9:32:35	One-A-Day Vitamins
9:33:05	Shell Oil
9:33:35	Ziploc Sandwich Bags
9:34:20	TWA
9:34:50	"Fatso" (Movie)
9:46:25	Silkience Hair Conditioner
9:46:55	Riunite Wine
9:57:45	Hertz Rent-A-Car
9:58:15	Wizard Deodorizer
9:58:45	Maybelline
9:59:15	Tostitos
10:00:00	Stella D'Oro Breadsticks
10:00:30	Hertz Rent-A-Car
10:12:10	L'Oreal Perfume
10:12:40	Emeraude Perfume
10:13:10	Milk Bone Dog Biscuits
10:13:40	Kotex
10:25:35	Columbian Coffee
10:26:05	Stresstabs
10:26:35	Liquid Plumber
10:27:05	"Sock Sense" (Movie)
10:27:55	American Airlines

10:28:55	Porsche
10:40:00	Bausch & Lomb Lenses
10:40:30	Flex Hair Conditioner
10:56:15	Pepsi Cola
10:56:45	Toyota
10:57:15	Aqua Fresh Toothpaste
10:57:45	Comtrex Cold Reliever
10:58:30	Citibank
11:13:35	Dexatrim
11:14:05	Wella Balsam Shampoo
11:14:35	Midatlantic Banks, Inc.
11:15:05	Sports Illustrated Magazine
11:15:35	Mazda
11:28:40	FILM ENDS
11:28:40	Contac
11:29:10	Theragran M
11:29:40	Progresso Spaghetti Sauce
11:30:10	Chase Bank
11:30:40	FILM CREDITS

Moreover, the creative effort and money that go into producing any one of these commercials is enormous compared to the costs of the programs which appear. A thirty-second spot will cost between $20,000 and $200,000 to make.[7] The true creativity of television is found in these commercials, which three out of four viewers say are "fun to watch."[8] A decade ago, actors began earning more money from commercials than from their appearances on television and in motion pictures combined.[9]

Beyond this, the underlying message of the commercial world, in the words of Erik Barnouw, the foremost historian on the subject of broadcasting in the United States, is that God's "work of Creation has been largely a disaster, functionally and aesthetically. Almost everything done in the making of man and his environment was a mistake; fortunately, man himself has invented products to correct the errors."[10]

Socialist societies, though freer from the dominance of such commercialism, have their own problems in relating to the creation. Technologies capable of serious environmental damage are embraced with little caution. Thus Cuba plans to build nuclear power plants, and the Soviet Union's energy policies, relying heavily on coal and nuclear energy, pose serious ecological stresses and risks.

In both of these ideological systems, economic growth is the chief value, and the economy is designed on the model of antagonism toward, and supremacy over, the creation.

Biblical insight suggests a different vision. For the church, we have seen how its economy is to reflect its ecology. This same truth applies to the whole household of the world. Economy and ecology must begin in reconciliation rather than in combat. Any society must be organized so that its economy cooperates with its ecology. As with the church, this holds true from the local to the global arena. The church's ecumenical economy, reflecting its ecology, is a vision for the world.

What might this look like? One economist who has worked hard to integrate economy and ecology is Herman Daly. He proposes a "steady-state" system of economics rooted in ecological realities. Daly writes, "Sufficient wealth efficiently maintained and allocated, and equitably distributed—not maximum production— is the proper economic aim."[11] He advocates an economics that recognizes the interdependence of creation, the limits of its resources, and a harmonious relationship between humanity and its environment.

The point is not to construct a "Christian economics" that secular society should unhesitantly embrace. Rather, the church's call is to offer practical ways in which biblical insight can stimulate alternatives in our economic vision and structures. Substantial reflection and experimentation is required. But a holistic understanding of economy and ecology is a fresh place to begin.

Land. The church can act to restore a land ethic among its members and to extend this sense of caring for the land into society. Attitudes, values, and priorities are what must initially be transformed. The uses of land should be determined not by the economic forces of the marketplace, but by the purposes for which God intends this gift to be utilized.

A variety of public policies at both the state and local levels of government have been employed in attempts to combat the loss of agricultural land. Such land use programs, however, cover less than 20 million of the 413 million acres presently farmed in the United States, and most existing laws have loopholes large enough for a bulldozer to drive through.

Tax incentives, zoning practices, and the purchase of "development rights" to keep land in farming are some of the other means that offer possibilities for averting the loss of farmland and bringing it under the control of forces other than the real estate market.

But preserving farmland acreage accomplishes little if agricultural practices attack and erode the soil. The increasing loss of soil through erosion raises fundamental questions concerning modern agricultural methods. Monoculture cropping with heavy tillage and massive inputs of chemical fertilizers is taking a serious toll on the structure and durability of the soil. Earthkeeping suggests that other alternative methods of agriculture, which are rooted in the care and preservation of the soil, must be adopted.

A recent memo by the head of the Farmers Home Administration stated: "Because of an imminent scarcity and eventual exhaustion of our natural resources, particularly fossil fuels, there is some concern for the heavy reliance by American agriculture on inorganic fertilizers and chemical pesticides, largely petroleum-based. . . . We recognize the (1) low energy intensiveness, (2) low potential for environmental damage, and (3) the feasibility of the producer to shift to conventional methods, as advantages of organic farming."

In 1980, a Department of Agriculture study came to the conclusion that there is little difference in crop yields between organic and inorganic farming. Further, the rising costs of chemical fertilizers and other products is equalizing the profit margin between the two.

However, extremely little research has been conducted by the Department of Agriculture and by land grant universities into such alternative agricultural techniques. In fact, a U.S. Senate subcommittee revealed that over half of the land grant universities actually discourage organic farming. But these very methods, including the planting of polycultural perennials (rather than monoculture annuals), hold the promise of reducing soil loss, preserving soil quality, and using less energy.

At the Land Institute in Salina, Kansas, Wes Jackson and others are working to model a "soft agriculture," which protects and nourishes the soil. Jackson believes that "sustainable culture must be rooted in sustainable agriculture." And modern agriculture, with its heavy tillage of the soil, its monocropping, and its reliance on oil and chemicals, cannot be sustained. Modern till agriculture, Jackson says, is a "global disease."

The Institute's research has focused on planting various polyculture plots of perennials.[12] In other words, seed-producing plants, which grow back each year and reseed themselves, are planted. They are grown not as one isolated variety (monoculture), but with other species (polyculture). Plants like the Eastern Gama-grass, a distant relative of corn with three times the protein, are studied.

The vision is that farmlands can be planted more like the prairies they originally destroyed. Instead of tearing up the ground each year to plant new monoculture annuals like corn and wheat, which cause inevitable erosion and soil destruction, fields would be cultivated with perennials—each yielding their harvest for gathering in due season, and ensuring the life of the soil. Tough analysis accompanies the Land Institute's work, and its results are an example of how a changed theology of the land can sow new seeds and reap a promising harvest.

As with few other issues, land raises directly the questions of ownership. Imbedded within Western culture, the right to own property, and especially land, has acquired a nearly sacred status. Yet, owning the soil of the ground as one's personal possession is foreign to many other cultures: moreover, biblical perspectives suggest a very different vision.

We have seen how the constant biblical theme points to God as the owner of creation and its resources. Nowhere is this more evident than with the land. The reference in Leviticus 25:23 cited earlier is but one example underscoring this truth: "The land shall not be sold in perpetuity, for the land is mine." The Bible never sanctions the idea that the land is one's private, personal possession, to be treated as one selfishly pleases. Rather, land is a gift, given to us on loan. Further, this loan comes not to individuals, but rather to God's people corporately.

Are there viable models in our own culture that respond to this vision? Fortunately, yes. Community land trusts are a concrete example. Land is purchased cooperatively and then placed in a trust and removed from the market. Participants have rights to cultivate the land—if the trust covers agricultural acreage—and to benefit from its fruits. Often, these rights may be granted for a lifetime, and can even be inherited. But the land itself is no longer a commodity to be bought and sold for a profit. Rather, it is a resource held corporately in trust for designated purposes.

Land trusts can be used for a variety of purposes—preserving open spaces, safeguarding wildlife habitat, or removing farmland from the real estate market. Further, the same concept has been extended to housing for the poor in the inner city. There, apartment buildings have been purchased and placed in a community trust. They are removed from the speculative real estate market, and become secure living places for those who dwell there.

The experience being gained by community land trusts all across the country is being documented. *Private Options: Tools and Concepts for Land Preservation,* published by the Montana Land Reliance and Trust Exchange, is the record of two national conferences held by four hundred local land trusts to exchange their ideas. And Rodale Press, which has long pioneered in publishing magazines and books about environmental concerns, has released *The Community Land Trust Handbook.* This book explains the basic idea of land trusts, examines eleven examples, both urban and rural, and gives practical hints for organizing such a venture. The church at all levels should learn from the growing experience of such land trusts.

Before slavery was abolished, the legal status of slaves had to be changed so they could be given rights as persons, rather than treated as property. Similarly, if land is to be cherished as a resource for all, its legal status also must undergo a dramatic transformation, and there must be recognition that it has inherent rights, to be held in trust for all people. Community land trusts are a small, yet hopeful step in this long journey. And we can pray that as with slavery, those voices crying out to respect the land would include many whose faith has given them a new vision of creation's sanctity.

Waste. The concept of waste and disposability grows out of humanity's alienated relationship to the creation. And the consequences of this distorted way of thinking are extremely damaging. Each year the United States spends over $4 billion just to collect and dispose of solid waste. And the land where so much of it has been buried is not only groaning, but is beginning to rebel. Groundwater pollution from landfills is increasingly common, as well as a host of other dangers that are present because what we throw away won't go away.

Ten percent of the U.S. energy supply ends up in products that are simply discarded. As one example, producing aluminum from recycled scrap uses 96 percent less energy than creating aluminum from ore.

Waste is a function of luxury. Poor societies are incredibly well advanced in recycling. India's garbage is perhaps the best sorted and reclaimed as any in the world, for the poor search through it for anything of value to use or sell. Even political posters in Calcutta are painted on walls rather than printed on paper, because posters would never remain on walls, but would be used for more practical purposes.

The affluent waste parts of all the earth's resources, not just what is thrown into the garbage. With little sense of our connection to creation, we are oblivious to daily practices made with the assumption that resources are limitless and disposable. In a modern hotel in Singapore, I was greeted with a sign on the bathroom sink that read: "Please Help Us to Conserve Water." It explained that getting good water there had not been easy, and urged brushing teeth with just a glass of water (saving 45 liters by not letting the tap run), washing hands and face with a half-full basin (18 liters saved), showering by turning the water only to rinse before and after soaping up (90 liters saved), and not taking a bath (110 liters saved).

In Grand Rapids, Michigan, a county-wide recycling project begun by concerned Christians wanting to develop appropriate technology has had amazing results. Recycle Unlimited uses a truck and trailer to pick up and process tin cans, aluminum, plastic, glass bottles and jars, newspapers, and brown bags at the curbside. The group has nurtured strong community cooperation and has had an impact on the country's solid-waste policies.

Part of the solution is to halt the flow of needless bottles, containers, and packaging that comes to us in the first place, particularly with our food. This is one contribution food cooperatives make, since they enable consumers to purchase food that has not gone through endless processing and packaging. In Missoula, Montana, my home church community has run the Good Food Store for several years, a retail store selling natural and whole foods in bulk, with a minimum of packaging and processing. Sales total over 600,000 dollars in a year.

This brief look at how a renewed biblical vision of creation and redemption can shape a response to various dimensions of the world's life is just a sample of the work of global sanctification. The possibilities for any local church body to become involved in such a ministry are endless.

In many key areas, new approaches can best take root at the local level. Furthering renewable energy, for example, can best be done through local efforts to rely more on decentralized energy sources. Many communities are doing energy studies to examine the economic and ecological costs of their energy consumption, and going to alternatives emphasizing conservation and renewable energy sources. Efforts at farmland preservation and soil conservation can be promoted through initiatives at the county level. The same is true of alternative approaches to solid waste. Overall land use planning is best implemented at the county level, usually with opportunities for citizen participation.

Christ came to save and heal the world. His Body can offer to the world models that reveal the connection of all the creation to God, and these could be the true hope for the world's healing. The whole creation, Paul reminds us, is waiting—waiting for the church to embark on its mission of global sanctification.

NOTES

1. Ghillean T. Prance, "Missionaries as Earthkeepers," *Radix,* November–December 1982, p. 23.
2. These are examples of the more discerning and valuable publications concerning theological and biblical perspectives on the nuclear arms race: Dale Aukerman, *Darkening Valley: A Biblical Perspective on Nuclear War* (New York: Seabury Press, 1981); Don Kraybill, *Facing Nuclear War: A Plea for Christian Witness* (Scottdale, Pa.: Herald Press, 1982); *A Matter of Faith: A Study Guide for Churches on the Nuclear Arms Race* (Washington, D.C.: Sojourners magazine, 1981); Richard Taylor and Ronald Sider, *Nuclear Holocaust and Christian Hope* (Downers Grove, Ill.: InterVarsity Press, 1982); Jim Wallis, *Waging Peace* (San Francisco: Harper & Row, 1982).
3. Jonathan Schell, *The Fate of the Earth* (New York: Alfred A. Knopf, 1982; New York: Avon Books, 1982), p. 111. Schell offers on pages 111–114 an insightful theological description of how humanity's development of nuclear arsenals has increased the power of death within the global ecosystem. Similar disucssion is also found on pages 123–130, and the ending paragraphs of Schell's book echo the biblical call for a choice between death and life, quoting Christ's words, "I come not to judge the world but to save it."
4. Ibid., p. 93.
5. "Looking Straight at the Bomb," *Time* magazine, 6 July 1981, p. 79.
6. Ibid. and other sources.
7. Erik Barnouw, *The Sponsor* (New York: Oxford University Press, 1978), p. 81.
8. Ibid., p. 80.
9. Ibid., p. 81.
10. Ibid., p. 96.
11. Larry L. Rasmussen, *Economic Anxiety and Christian Faith* (Minneapolis: Augsburg Publishing Company, 1981), p. 18. Herman Daly's thought is outlined in the book he edited, *Toward a Steady-State Economy* (San Francisco: W. H. Freeman and Co., 1973) and in Herman Daly, *Steady-State Economics* (San Francisco: W. H. Freeman and Company, 1977).
12. A summary of the Land Institute's vision is found in Wes Jackson's *New Roots for Agriculture* (San Francisco: Sierra Club Books, 1981). The Institute's work is also summarized in its publication *The Land Report,* available three times a year from The Land Institute, Rte. 2, Salina, Kansas 67401.

12. Authoring Life

The publisher of *U.S. News and World Report* introduced a recent cover article on biotechnology this way:

No longer do (scientists) have to wait for nature to provide the combination of genetic traits they want in microbes, plants, animals—even human beings. They can simply splice new genes into cells to create the organisms they want.[1]

While the church's stand against the nuclear ability to destroy created life has become more steadfast each day, its response to the technological ability to create new life has been weak, ambiguous, and muted. Yet equally profound dangers are present. Furthermore, important theological judgments about the integrity of life are being made by researchers in universities and corporations. These are going largely unnoticed by the church.

In fact, the most alarming features in the revolution of biotechnology are not its scientific advances but its theological assumptions. The capabilities of genetic engineering underscore humanity's absolute power over the authorship of life and its temporal sovereignty as ruler over the creation.

As biotechnology has conferred on humanity an undreamed-of power to create new life forms, the church has remained passive. The theological justification of humanity's domination of nature has gone unexamined and unamended. A Presidential commission on bioethics, requested by three church denominations to explore the moral issues in genetic engineering, offered little new theological insight in its 1982 report: "Human beings have not merely the right but the duty to employ their God-given powers to harness nature for human benefit."[2] Its recommendations for genetic engineering amounted to little more than a weak "be careful." The *New York Times* correctly chastised the report for having "tiptoed around the more concrete issues,"[3] such as altering the human gene set.

Meanwhile, society's technological euphoria over genetic engineering has smothered already faint theological and moral qualms. Cover stories in *Time* and *Newsweek,* as well as reports on television newscasts, all stress the amazing prospects for rescuing the U.S. economy as well as for solving the energy crisis and revolutionizing agriculture, which genetic engineering could bring. Such media coverage echoes the stories in 1945–46 describing how the harnessing of nuclear power would revolutionize transportation, make energy limitless, and even control the weather.[4]

Society's hope for a technological fix to its economic, environmental, and resource problems now rests on genetic engineering. The root causes of economic stagnation, ecological deterioration, and resource scarcity can all be remedied, it is believed, by the purely technical solutions provided by genetic engineering.

The church's response to all these developments must be other than a shallow and a blanket condemnation of modern technology. Rather, we should examine how biblical insights can shape a response that illumines the dangers being courted by society and clarifies our concrete choices.

First, the biblical directive to care for the creation assumes a relationship of cooperation and involvement with it. Arguing against interfering with the "natural order" misses the point. Humanity's life is never separate from the rest of creation, but intrinsically tied to it. As we have seen, the Bible calls us to care for rather than exploit the creation. Ownership is the central question, and Scripture declares that creation is God's and not ours.

Wearing eyeglasses, growing tomatoes, taking aspirin, and eating three meals a day all involve some attempt to effect the "natural order." Genetic engineering begins in its mildest forms as another such attempt. Some of its results, such as inexpensive insulin, improved treatment of burns, and various vaccines, will indeed by beneficial in the short run. Rather than issuing abstract warnings against any tampering with nature, the church should

examine how various possibilities of genetic engineering affect the
relationship between humanity, creation, and God.

Practitioners of genetic engineering have generally been suspi-
cious of moral, ethical, and theological discussions of their activities. They often stand behind the classic defense of scientific inquiry. Society, and especially religion, they claim, must not
attempt to limit the scope of their investigation.

But the matter is not that simple. In unique ways, genetic engineering welds together science and technology in such a way that
there are immediate effects on nature. New variations and forms
of life are created and introduced into the ecosystem. This goes
beyond free inquiry, to the creation of new facts and new relationships in the world of nature.

Similarly, proponents of biotechnology often declare that one
cannot stand in the way of scientific and technological progress. If
something can be done, then it should be done, and will be done
anyway, regardless of reservations. This thinking further enslaves
us to the technological process.

It is foolhardy to give technology a free hand. The possibilities
of genetic engineering should make this self-evident. As one
physician and scientist has said, "We must get used to the idea that
biomedical technology makes possible many things we should
never do."[5]

Historically, the impetus for pushing any technology to the extremes of potential human destructiveness has come from the military. Today, we can assume that in some top secret laboratories
and think-tanks in our land, people are researching how the tools
and potential creations of genetic engineering could be used
against the nation's enemies.

Since General Electric has now patented a micro-organism that
can eat up the oil from a tanker spill, why not develop a strategy
for unleashing it in the Soviet Union's oil fields?

Why not create a micro-organism capable of carrying behavior-
modifying drugs, in an undetectable manner, to Soviet military
personnel and strategic planners?

What about a new microbe which would rust Nicaragua's military equipment in just a few days?

Why not cross human genes with an animal and breed a new organism not quite human that could be programmed with a bio-chip to carry out military instructions unto death?

And shouldn't there be a small number of genetically engineered humans with super-intelligence, raised under careful military supervision, and devoted to spending their lives thinking of strategies to outwit the nation's enemies?

We should assume that bizarre possibilities like these are being contemplated and evaluated as part of military research. Once society uncritically blesses the advance of genetic engineering, its manipulation for military purposes accelerates without any restraint. Eventually, as with nuclear power, it will become difficult to separate military applications from civilian uses. The church should sound the warning about these dangers.

Public developments in genetic engineering are being driven by their profit-making potential. Here again, as with nuclear power, the hope of economic returns discounts the inherent risks in the technology. The immediate, short-run benefits that appear to be humane are embraced, while the long-term dangers to the genetic and ecological balance of life are ignored.

When recombinant DNA technology first emerged, there was concern that new micro-organisms might accidentally escape into the outside world. Since they can live in a human intestine and even in sewage, the threat of a new biological creation on the loose was enough to impose a temporary moratorium on such research. It was lifted, however, when the federal government and the scientists whose careers depended on biotechnology created safety standards for such research. Argument has continued over whether these standards are sufficient. Whether or not they are is beside the point, since they are only mandatory where the federal government funds the research—corporations are not obligated to follow them. And with profit as the goal, such safeguards become tempting obstacles to be quietly bypassed.

The creations of genetic engineering that are designed to live outside laboratories also pose risks to the ecosystem. When General Electric's microbes gobble up the oil spilled by a tanker, then what do they do? What if they don't dissolve as planned? What if they enter the ecosystem of the ocean permanently—an ecosystem designed neither to injest spilled oil nor to accommodate invented predators of oil slicks?

A unique biohazard is created by such pollution, for the source is a living organism that reproduces itself. Cleaning up such biological pollution means trying to blot out a whole new life form.

Biotechnology has no intention of stopping with the creation of a few new industrially useful microbes. Rapidly, it is moving up the scale of life, even developing the potential ability to create whole new species. Far more than simply breeding hybrids is involved.

In 1981, scientists successfully transferred a rabbit gene into a mouse embryo, and the newborn mouse (with a little bit of rabbit) successfully mated. Reprogramming a whole species thus became possible by transferring distinct traits of one animal to another.

For example, certain traits of a buffalo, such as its preference for grass as opposed to costly feed grain, could be transferred to a breed of cattle. Further, the corporation that produced such a buffalo-cow could claim a patent and ownership on every such buffalo-cow that was ever born. The Supreme Court's 1980 decision opening the way for corporations to patent new life forms reflects how deeply society believes that creation is ours to possess.

The point, of course, is not whether animals should serve humans. Modifying animal breeds as well as nurturing plant varieties has long been done. But genetic engineering presents wholly novel possibilities. One species can now be altered by incorporating the traits of another. Species boundaries are no longer inviolate, but can be crossed at will. Even new species of life could be brought into existence—and all to satisfy economic whims.

Instead of seeing a given species as an established and purposeful part of creation's order, the genetic engineer sees simply a genetic program at work. That program can be modified, reworked, and altered in any way deemed useful—the life of a species compels no inherent respect. It is merely a particular programming of information. Genetic engineering gives humanity access to the keyboard for writing whole new programs.

What would be the likely consequences if humanity so controlled and dominated the variation of life's species?

The bald eagle, rainbow trout, the grizzly bear, and lady bugs would have no intrinsic value. Their worth would depend only on their commercial, recreational, or aesthetic value to humans. And the limitations or defects of any one species could be remedied by genetically reprogramming them.

Such dominion jeopardizes the life of all creation. Choosing to create new life forms constitutes an unprecedented invasion of the life-sustaining fabric of creation. The likely loss of genetic diversity—which is already occurring from the increased extinction of species due to human causes—would dwindle creation's ability to nurture future life.

Science fiction has long imagined mechanical robots serving humans. But science is making possible the development of an endless variety of life forms—not machines—to serve as our slaves. One unnoticed dimension of biotechnology is its eventual fusion with computer technology. Biochips created through genetic engineering will replace microchips, and enable programming and computer-like functioning to be built into new forms of life.

Authoring species seems better entrusted to God. When Noah took two of every "kind" of animal into the ark, he responded to humanity's calling to uphold the created order. This was affirmed in God's covenant after the flood which extended to all living creatures. Such passages suggest a biblical integrity in all species of life and an inherent value that stems from their relationship to the Creator rather than to humanity.

Species, of course, are not eternal. Some become extinct, and others arise, in the aeons of creation's life. But the wisdom behind those changes belongs to the Creator. Humanity's task is one of preservation. Our energies are more faithfully exercised through nurturing and protecting present species rather than presuming to rearrange their genes. Crossing species lines in the creation of new forms of life amounts to a new form of technological blasphemy.

The final frontier in genetic engineering is the re-creation of humanity's genetic characteristics. Biotechnology is providing the tools for designing human life according to predetermined specifications. Humans are about to acquire the power of authorship over human life itself.

This power is rationalized with the promise of curing hereditary diseases and correcting genetic flaws. Presently such efforts are focused on genetic surgery to change certain conditions within an embryo or an individual. Whatever their value or risk, such changes die with the person—nothing is passed on to future generations.

The next step, however, is to change such defects through engineering the germline cells—the egg and sperm—of individuals. And these changes, of course, are inheritable. They permanently alter the human germline, which is the storehouse for sustaining the future of the human species.

Correcting "defective" genes in this manner poses grave biological and moral dangers. The strength of any species is tied to its genetic diversity; genes we may judge to be "bad" may, in fact, have an unknown but indispensable redemptive role in humanity's genetic adaptability and preservation. Removing unwanted genetic traits could cause unpredictable injury to humanity's genetic composition and cripple its ability to adapt to dramatic changes in its environment.

Moreover, the whole idea of changing inheritable defective genes and disorders presumes that humanity can be genetically perfected. It rests on a faith in humanity's capacity to recreate ourselves in our own image. Eliminating a hereditary disease may seem clear-cut and humane. But the genetic engineering of human life goes a far distance beyond such simplistic choices.

No sharp line can be drawn between changing genetic defects and enhancing genetic characteristics. The idea of "defects" depends, after all, on the possibility of being "perfect." If the "flaw" of diabetes or sickle cell anemia can be corrected, then why not change the imperfections of bad looks, lefthandedness, or skin color? Why not improve brains or temperament? As the *New York Times* editorialized, "There is no discernible line to be drawn between making inheritable repairs of genetic defects, and improving the species."[6]

The ability of genetic engineering to program mental and psychological functioning unleashes the power for molding a society to fit the norms of its rulers. Why not genetically eliminate social misfits? Why not genetically reinforce passive, conforming personality characteristics? Many regimes would find it tantilizing to reinforce their rule and quiet dissent through genetic control on its citizens rather than through external force.

Such dangers may seem far-fetched, especially in pluralistic societies. But in capitalistic countries like the United States, genetic control would first be established not by the state, but by the marketplace. Every parent wants a perfect baby. If there are gene banks offering a variety of desired traits, people will pay to perfect their offspring.

Since wealth and power will determine who will have access to such choices, economic divisions would be genetically reinforced. Those with wealth would strive to improve their genetic riches. The end result would be a new basis for discrimination, inequality, and oppression based no longer on race or class, but on genetic composition. A virtual biological caste system could result.

From Auschwitz to Hiroshima to Love Canal, humanity has decisively demonstrated that its technological powers overwhelm its capacities for moral judgment. The genetic engineering of human life, if allowed to proceed, will quickly trespass any well-intentioned boundaries and guidelines. This technology is setting its own rules and tempting humanity with awesome powers. If grasped, such power will become intoxicating, and the pressure to seize all of it will be irresistible.

Humanity neither knows enough about the intricacies of life, nor possesses the moral discernment and spiritual wisdom to design "more perfect" human beings. Such actions claim prerogatives for humanity that rightly belong only to the Creator.

On this last point, the church's voice is beginning to be heard.

In the middle of 1983, a unified group of church leaders spoke out in opposition to the genetic engineering of the human germline. The group included evangelicals such as Carl F. H. Henry, Pat Robertson, John Perkins, Ted Engstrom, Jim Wallis, and Jerry Falwell. Leaders of almost every mainline protestant denomination were also signers of the statement, including former National Council of Churches President James Armstrong, theologian J. Robert Nelson, United Church of Christ head Avery Post, former Reformed Church in America General Secretary Arie Brouwer (now with the World Council of Churches), and many others. Several leading Catholic bishops—liberal and conservative—also joined. This was as theologically diverse a group of religious leaders responding to a major social question as has been seen in recent decades.

Their concise statement, calling on Congress to legislate against genetically designing humans, ignited widespread discussion, which still continues. The church has begun to confront the theological pretensions inherent in genetic engineering.

Opposition to the genetic engineering of human beings, however, is only a starting point for the church's response. The technological ability to author new life forms at any level compels humanity to decide whether it is the source, guide, and goal of life, or whether those attributes belong to the Creator, as suggested by Paul in Romans 11:36. The consistent biblical word calling humanity to preserve and treasure created life, which was given as God's gift, should restrain humanity from trying to reprogram the genetic makeup of creation.

Paul wrote to the church at Corinth, "Do you not know that your body is a shrine of the indwelling Holy Spirit, and the Spirit is God's gift to you? You do not belong to yourselves; you were bought at a price. Then honour God in your body" (1 Corinthians 6:20). This New Testament insight declares that we do not own ourselves. Even our own bodies are not ours to possess, and that includes our genes, as well as creation's genetic composition.

Growing up as an evangelical, I often heard verses declaring that our bodies were the temples of God quoted as the reason for not smoking. More relevant applications spring to mind today. For it we are to regard our bodies and all creation not as our own, but as the place where God dwells, then their genetic design rightly remains in God's hands rather than our own.

NOTES

1. *U.S. News and World Report,* 28 March 1983, p. 4.
2. "Splicing Life: A Report on the Social and Ethical Issues of Genetic Engineering with Human Beings," published by the President's Commission for the Study of Ethical Problems in Medicine and Biomedical Research, 1982, p. 56. At about the same time the Presidential Commission released its report, the National Council of Churches' Panel on Bioethical Concerns issued a study paper that began to raise some of the important issues involved in human genetic engineering, but it received very little attention.
3. "The Rules for Reshaping Life," *New York Times,* 29 December 1982.
4. See, for example, Daniel Ford, *The Cult of the Atom* (New York: Simon and Schuster, 1982), pp. 29–31.
5. Leon Kass, "The New Biology; What Price Reducing Man's Estate?" *Science* 174 (1971): 779, quoted in a footnote to "Splicing Life," p. 59.
6. "Whether to Make Perfect Humans," *New York Times,* 22 July 1982, p. A22.

Postscript

We are left to encounter the question of death, and how death is seen in light of creation and redemption. The traditional interpretation, taken in general from Romans 4:25, is that "death entered the world through sin." Because of these words, many have thought that before the disobedience of Adam, physical death did not exist in creation, that with the onset of sin all creation became subject to mortality, and that those called by God will be saved from such mortality in eternity, where death will be no more.

This view is adequate as long as humanity is kept separate from the rest of creation, and that is our tendency: we deepen humanity's separation by our belief that death reigns in the world but that humanity will be freed from death by being saved out of this world. This quickly becomes a gnostic heresy, however, assuming an inherent dualism in creation of an evil world opposed by a righteous God.

Such a traditional view presents other difficulties as well. First, how could physical death in all of nature, apart from humanity, result from sin? We encounter a biological problem here, for it requires the belief that no death in nature existed prior to the sin of Adam and Eve. Some theologians, assuming that the Genesis account was literal history, argue that since the animals were created on the same day as humanity, they all could have gone on living, without death. But once humanity sinned, they too were subject to death.

While such a view may have appeared plausible three centuries ago, it does not today. How could the animal world, in all of its forms, exist without physical death—even for a few hours? Could every ant avoid being stepped on by an elephant? Could every fly dodge the sweep of a cow's tail? Did no bee sting before the fall? Additionally, thinking that death in nature is a function of sin assumes that predation—one animal eating another; a trout eating a salmon fly—could not exist apart from sin. But how then could most animal species survive?

If we are to be consistent, the same truths we apply to the animal world must also apply to plants, which are just as much a part of the life of nature. Maintaining that no plant life died until humanity sinned—or that plants don't live forever because of sin—becomes nonsensical. And according to Genesis, Adam and Eve were eating before their sin, which, if one wishes to take this story as historical fact, means that at least some plants were dying.

Finally, making such an assumption about death in nature raises theological difficulties. Why should humanity's disobedience cause God to punish every creature and plant ever created? What kind of a God would visit such relentless punishment on every organism in the creation?

Certainly creation suffers because of humanity's sin—because of humanity's persistent misuse of creation, which, as we said earlier, spreads injury like an infection into the nonhuman creation. But that is not to claim that God is the author of biological death in nature as a punishment. The fall is not a biological fact of creation.

If death within creation—meaning the death of biological organisms—is not a result of human sin, it must have been present from the beginning of creation. Biological death, then, is part of the *goodness* of creation. The cosmos, the world, and all within it, pronounced "good" or "right" even before the advent of humanity, was created by God to include biological death.

An ecological understanding of creation lends insight into what at first seems to be outlandish—God's creation of death. Every living organism, we discover, is given life because of death. It survives because some other part of creation has relinquished its life. The trout lives because the stone fly dies. The osprey lives because the trout dies. You and I live because countless plants and animals die.

The world of nature is bound inseparably through this web of life and death. We are, quite literally, members one of another. Even within organisms, the death of cells makes possible the birth of new cells. Growth does not simply end in death; it is *enabled* by death.

Within any ecosystem, death within its parts makes possible its overall life. If all organisms in an ecosystem simply multiplied without restraint, life for the whole would be impossible; life-giving resources would quickly be exhausted. Humanity's intervention in ecosystems is full of examples where attempts to limit one species have led to the explosion of another species, upsetting the previous balance.

So at every level—from within the cellular life of organisms, to relationships between organisms, to the overall life of ecosystems—life is made possible by death. We can say that this is part of the Creator's intention.

Such insights are by no means foreign to Scripture. Our exploration of the Bible has revealed numerous passages that draw on the life within the creation for spiritual insight. The seed must die before life sprouts forth, just as we must lose our lives to find them. And not even a sparrow falls, apart from God's knowledge and sovereignty. Moreover, biblical passages (such as Psalm 104 and parts of Job) describe animals being provided to predators as part of God's provision, within the design of creation.

What might it mean to be practically instructed by such insight? Take, for example, eating, composting, and gardening. We persist in thinking that elements of the nonhuman creation can be used, and the leftovers thrown away. But the orange peels, the watermelon rinds, the cow manure, the grass clippings, and the fallen leaves all carry the potential of life within their own decay. When allowed to decompose, mixed with some soil with its various organisms, its death in fact becomes a source of life as compost, which gives the earth the nutrients it needs. This soil can produce a rich harvest of vegetables and fruits that make life possible for other living things. Death and decay, then, become not an unwanted end of life, but a redemptive means for nurturing life. Organic versus inorganic agriculture becomes a theological question.

Yet there are biblical passages that point to an end of predation within nature, a harmony within the animal world that is part of God's redemptive work. In Isaiah 11, for instance, we read that "the wolf will lie down with the kid," and "the lion will eat straw like the ox." How are we to interpret these passages?

First, they do not indicate a return to the idyllic state of Eden. The Bible does not view the future primarily as a return to some previously ideal world. Rather, God's redemptive purposes bring about a new and redeemed future. They restore and fulfill God's purposes in creation—making what can be called a *new* creation. Passages such as those in Isaiah indicate that this newness will extend even to the functioning of relationships between animals. How this will operate biologically seems ultimately beyond our imagination.

All of this does not mean that the initial goodness of creation will be destroyed. In the process of redemption, God can take what was created good, but later injured by human rebellion, and fashion a new reality beyond our comprehension, one that witnesses in all fullness to God's perfect love.

How, then, does all this relate to death for humanity? Here we encounter even more challenging theological issues. First, is humanity's biological death a result of its sin? This would seem, on the surface, to be the message of Genesis 2–3, as well as of Paul's reflections on these matters in Romans 4. Yet there are some anomalies that are not accounted for, and these should push our reflection further.

First, in Genesis 2:17, the warning is given that if Adam and Eve eat of the forbidden fruit, then "*on that day* [they] will surely die." However, they do not die physically or biologically on that day. In fact, they live a long life and, according to the account, begin the entire human race.

This raises the whole question of what the Bible means by "death," an issue already brought to light by Christ. His words in John 3:16, whoever "has faith in him may not die, but have eternal life," obviously do not eliminate the reality of physical death for us—or even for him. Likewise, when Paul declares that "death is swallowed up in victory" (1 Corinthians 15:54), again this does not abolish biological death for anyone.

We all die, and even Christ's victory over death does not erase our biological mortality. Might this suggest, then, that humanity's sin is not punished by biological death, but rather by a falling away from God, another sort of "death"? Could it be that humanity too was created mortal, like the rest of creation? Further, could eternal fellowship with God, which is restored through Christ's resurrection, have been the intended stage to follow biological death, before the entrance of sin? In other words, can we believe that the goodness of creation originally included humanity's biological death, which ushered in an eternal fellowship with the Creator?

Humanity's sin, as presented in Genesis, is the desire "to be like God," claiming our own authority over our lives. We separate ourselves from God, proclaiming our selfish sovereignty over life and creation. Such a reign is fatally threatened, however, by death, for the very fact of our physical death means the certain end to our self-rule. While desiring to be like God, we cannot conquer death, so it becomes our enemy. Having divorced ourselves from God, death consigns us to this spiritual separation, eternally.

In this fashion, death comes to mean, biblically, the state of separation from God. It is a condition of living in the present, as well as a threatened final destruction. In this way, sin and death become joined, and are seen biblically as almost one. Sin is the intent to live life apart from God, and death describes the alienation that follows.

Physical death, the ultimate threat to a self-sufficient life, holds us in bondage through fear. In this fashion, the Bible pictures death as having dominion over us. The powers and principalities that attempt to construct their reign over creation promise us power and fulfillment in our search to be our own gods. But they hold us captive through our fear of death. Our security is protected and sought at all costs; and in this attempt to fend off physical death, we threaten others and all creation with such death.

Captured by these powers—this alienation from God—humanity in turn lashes out at the creation, threatening and causing biological death. Pollutants in the air and water spread cancer in humans. Wasted water, eroded soil, and hoarded land cause malnutrition and hunger for the powerless. And preparations for biological and nuclear warfare threaten creation with destruction.

Sin has made physical death our enemy. As Paul expresses it, "The sting of death is sin" (1 Corinthians 15:56). Understood in this fashion, natural death, in and of itself, is not the enemy. Rather, death becomes the enemy when it separates us from God through the power of sin. While biological death is a part of God's creation, sin turns such death into an occasion for evil to unleash its power.

This dominion of sin and death was broken by Jesus Christ. The offering of himself, as God's Son, on the cross, defeated the power of death: death could not hold Christ captive. The threat of physical death did not deter his faithfulness to God; sin could not grasp his life. The ultimate weapon of the powers and principalities—death—was defeated by Christ at the cross. In this way, Christ "disarmed" the powers and principalities. All this was affirmed by Christ's resurrection.

Christ's victory is won for all the creation. The power of sin and death over our lives is broken. Death as the state of separation from God is defeated. And physical death thus loses its threat and "sting," for it ceases to separate us from God. No longer is death an enemy; no longer do we seek to fend off death in order to protect our self-rule. Instead, we proclaim Jesus as Lord. Our lives are not our own. And we are secure in the knowledge that "nothing in death or life, . . . nothing in all creation . . . can separate us from the love of God in Christ Jesus our Lord" (Romans 8:38–39).

Still, with physical death comes the anguish and pain of bereavement. And a death that seems, from the perspective of one who loved and was loved, to be untimely, feels remote from God's good creation. But even here, the words of biblical faith comfort us precisely by reminding us that even those whom we love most are not ours to possess. Like the rest of creation, they too belong not to us, but to God. "The Lord gives, and the Lord takes away. Blessed be the name of the Lord."

Through Christ, death is no longer separation. Rather, it becomes the pathway to life. Our own physical death is not the end of a solitary, self-governed existence, but a final step in our journey toward God. Life springs forth out of death.

More pointedly, the path of self-offering, of giving, of pouring out, of serving—this becomes the way for life to be nurtured in our daily pilgrimage. We are united to a love that gives itself away in the service of all creation. Just as life at all levels of the creation is possible only because of death, so for us the way of sacrifice and service brings forth life—to ourselves, to others, and to all creation.

We see in Christ the one who, through giving of his own life, restored all creation to God. And we see him as the force sustaining all creation. The creation lives, at all levels, through the giving up of life. The outstretched arms of Christ on the cross display the love that upholds every part of the creation.

That same love unites us to the creation. One with Christ, we are participants in the outpoured love that sustains all life. And our lives, transformed into parts of Christ's body, become the redemptive servants of creation.

Bibliography

Adams, Jennifer A. *The Solar Church*. New York: The Pilgrim Press, 1982.

A Matter of Faith: A Study Guide for Churches on the Nuclear Arms Race. Washington, D.C.: *Sojourners* magazine, 1981.

Anderson, Bernhard W. "The Earth Is the Lord's." *Interpretation* 9, no. 1 January 1955: 3–20.

Ashley, Maryle. *Keeping a Money Journal*. Germantown, Md.: Ministry of Money, Inc., January 1982.

Aukerman, Dale. *Darkening Valley: A Biblical Perspective on Nuclear War*. New York: Seabury Press, 1981.

Barbour, Ian G., ed. *Western Man and Environmental Ethics*. Menlo Park, Calif.: Addison-Wesley Publishing House, 1973.

Barfield, Owen. *Saving the Appearances*. New York: Harcourt Brace Jovanovich and London: Faber & Faber, 1957.

Barnette, Henlee H. *The Church and the Ecological Crisis*. Grand Rapids, Mich.: Eerdmans Publishing House, 1972.

Barnouw, Erik. *The Sponsor*. New York: Oxford University Press, 1978.

Bennett, Dennis, and Bennett, Rita. *The Holy Spirit and You*. Plainfield, N.J.: Logos International, 1971.

Berry, Wendell. *The Unsettling of America*. New York: Avon, 1977.

Birch, Bruce C., and Rasmussen, Larry L. *The Predicament of the Prosperous*. Philadelphia: The Westminster Press, 1978.

Bria, Ian, ed. *Jesus Christ—The Life of the World*. Geneva: The World Council of Churches, 1982.

Brueggemann, Walter. *Interpretation: Genesis*. Atlanta: John Knox Press, 1983.

Brueggemann, Walter. *The Land*. Philadelphia: Fortress Press, 1977.

Cesaretti, C. A., and Commins, Stephne. *Let the Earth Bless the Lord*. New York: Seabury Press, 1981.

Clouse, Robert G., ed. *The Meaning of the Millennium*. Downers Grove, Ill.: Inter-Varsity Press, 1977.

Daly, Herman. *Steady-State Economics*. San Francisco: W. H. Freeman and Co., 1977.

Daly, Herman, ed. *Toward a Steady-State Economy*. San Francisco: W. H. Freeman and Co., 1983.

Deloria, Vine, Jr. *God Is Red*. New York: Delta Publishing Co., 1973.

Dubos, René. *The Wooing of Earth*. New York: Charles Scribner's Sons, 1980.

Dumas, Andre. "The Creation—God's Glory in His World." *The Reformed World* 34, no. 7–8 September-December 1977: 311–315.

Dumas, Andre. "The Ecological Crisis and the Doctrine of Creation." *The Ecumenical Review* 27, no. 1 January 1975: 24–35.

Elder, Frederick. *Crisis in Eden*. Nashville: Abingdon, 1970.

Elsdon, Ron. *Bent World*. Downers Grove, Ill.: Inter-Varsity Press, 1981.

Empty Breadbasket? The Cornucopia Project. Emmaus, Pa.: Rodale Press, 1981.

Ford, Daniel. *The Cult of the Atom*. New York: Simon and Schuster, 1982.

Foster, Richard J. *Freedom of Simplicity*. San Francisco: Harper & Row, 1981.

Gardner, W. H., and MacKenzie, N. H., eds. *The Poems of Gerard Manley Hopkins*. London: Oxford University Press, 1967.

Gilkey, Langdon. *Maker of Heaven and Earth*. Garden City, N.Y.: Doubleday and Company, 1959.

Glacken, Clarence J. *Traces on the Rhodian Shore*. Berkeley and Los Angeles: University of California Press, 1967.

Gray, Elizabeth Dodson. *Green Paradise Lost*. Wellesley, Mass: Roundtable Press, 1979.

Gregorios, Paulos. *The Human Presence*. Geneva: The World Council of Churches, 1978.

Grosheide F. W. "The First Epistle to the Corinthians." *The New International Commentary on the New Testament*. Grand Rapids, Mich.: Eerdmans Publishing Co., 1953.

Hamilton, Michael, ed. *This Little Planet*. New York: Charles Scribner's Sons, 1970.

Harper, Michael. *A New Way of Living*. Plainfield, N.J.: Logos International, 1956.

Hendry, George S. "The Eclipse of Creation." *Theology Today* 28, no. 4 January 1972: 406–425.

Hendry, George S. *Theology of Nature*. Philadelphia: The Westminister Press, 1982.

Howard, Ted, and Rifkin, Jeremy. *Who Shall Play God?* New York: Dell Publishing Co., 1977.

Hughes, Philip E. "The Second Epistle to the Corinthians." *The New International Commentary on the New Testament*. Grand Rapids, Mich.: Eerdmans Publishing Co., 1962.

Hughes, Philip E., "The Doctrine of Creation in Hebrews 11:3." *Biblical Theology Bulletin* 2, no. 1 February 1972: 64–77.

Institute for Community Economics. *The Community Land Trust Handbook*. Rodale Press, 1982.

Inter-Lutheran Commission on Worship. *Contemporary Worship Services: The Holy Communion*. Minneapolis: Augsburg Publishing House, 1970.

Jackson, Wes. *New Roots for Agriculture*. San Francisco: Sierra Club Books, 1981.

Jegen, Mary Evelyn, and Manno, Bruno, eds. *The Earth Is the Lord's*. New York: Paulist Press, 1978.

Kraybill, Don. *Facing Nuclear War: A Plea for Christian Witness*. Scottdale, Pa.: Herald Press, 1982.

Longacre, Doris Janzen. *Living More with Less*. Scottdale, Pa.: Herald press, 1980.

Merchant, Carolyn. *The Death of Nature*. San Francisco: Harper and Row, 1980.

Montana Land Reliance and Land Trust Exchange. *Private Options: Tools and Concepts for Land Conservation*. Island Press, Calif. 1982.

O'Connor, Elizabeth. *Letters to Scattered Pilgrims*. San Francisco: Harper & Row, 1979.

Passmore, John. *Man's Responsibility for Nature*. New York: Charles Scribner's Sons, 1974.

Pulkingham, Graham W. *Gathered for Power*. New York: Morehouse-Barlow Co., 1972. Distributed by Logos International, Plainfield, N.J.

Pulkingham, Graham W. *They Left Their Nets*. New York: Morehouse-Barlow Co., 1973. Distributed by Logos International, Plainfield, N.J.

Rasmussen, Larry L. *Economic Anxiety and Christian Faith*. Minneapolis: Augsburg Publishing Co., 1981.

Reumann, John. *Creation and New Creation*. Minneapolis: Augsburg Publishing House, 1973.

Rifkin, Jeremy. *Algeny*. New York: Viking Press, 1983.

Rifkin, Jeremy. *Entropy*. New York: Viking Press, 1080.

Rifkin, Jeremy. *The Emerging Order*. New York: G. P. Putnam's Sons, 1979.

Robinson, Wheeler H. *Inspiration and Revelation in the Old Testament*. Oxford: The Clarendon Press, 1953.

Rust, Eric C. *Nature-Garden or Desert?* Waco, Tex.: Word Books, 1971.

Santmire, Paul H. *Brother Earth*. New York: Thomas Nelson, Inc., 1970.

Schaeffer, Francis A. *Pollution and the Death of Man*. Wheaton, Ill.: Tyndale, 1970.

Schell, Jonathan. *The Fate of the Earth*. New York: Alfred A. Knopf, 1982 and New York: Avon Books, 1982.

Schmemann, Alexander. *For the Life of the World*. St. Vladimir's Seminary press, 1973.

Shaw, D. W. "Process Thought and Creation." *Theology* 78, no. 661 (July, 1975): 346–355.

Sider, Ronald, and Taylor, Richard. *Nuclear Holocaust and Christian Hope*. Downers Grove, Ill.: Inter-Varsity Press, 1982.

Sittler, Joseph. *Essays on Nature and Grace*. Philadelphia: Fortress Press, 1972.

Snow, Catherine. *Writing a Money Autobiography*. Germantown, Md.: Ministry of Money, Inc., Jan. 1983.

Snyder, Howard A. *Liberating the Church*. Downers Grove, Ill.: Inter-Varsity Press, 1983.

Squiers, Edwin R., ed. *The Environmental Crisis: The Ethical Dilemma*. Mancelona, Mich.: The AuSable Trails Institute of Environmental Studies, 1980.

Steck, Odil Hannes. *World and Environment*. Nashville: Abingdon, 1980.

Steffenson, Dave; Herrscher, Walter J.; and Cook, Robert S. eds., *Ethics for Environment: Three Religious Strategies*. Green Bay, Wis.: UWBG Ecumenical Center, 1973.

Stone, Glenn C., ed. *A New Ethic for a New Earth*. Faith-Man-Nature Group: Friendship Press, 1971.

Taylor, John V. *Enough Is Enough*. London: SCM Press, 1975.

Tedlock, Dennis, and Tedlock, Barbara, eds. *Teachings from the American Earth*. New York: Liveright, 1975.

Wallis, Jim. *Waging Peace*. San Francisco: Harper & Row, 1982.

Ward, Miriam, ed. *Biblical Studies in Contemporary Thought*. Somerville, Mass.: Grenno, Hadden & Company, Ltd., 1975.

Westermann, Claus. *Creation*. Philadelphia: Fortress Press, 1974.

Wilkinson, Loren, ed. *Earthkeeping*. Grand Rapids, Mich.: Eerdmans Publishing Co., 1980.

Wolfson, Harry A. "The Identification of Ex Nihilo with Emanation in Gregory of Nyssa." *Harvard Theological Review* 63 (1970): 53–60.

Yoder, John Howard. *The Christian Witness to the State*. Institute of Mennonite Studies, vol. 3. Newton, Kans.: Faith and Life Press, 1964.

Yoder, John Howard. *The Politics of Jesus*. Grand Rapids, Mich.: Eerdmans Publishing Co., 1972.

Young, Norman. *Creator, Creation and Faith*. Philadelphia: Westminister Press, 1978.

Index